Night in Hostel No.7

I0560498

by
Ramesh Patnaik

VIDYA
PUBLISHING INC.

Vidya Publishing Inc.
Toronto, Canada || Bhubaneswar, Odisha

Night in Hostel No.7

Author : Ramesh Patnaik

....

ISBN : 978-1-998475-86-5

Copyright © 2025 by Ramesh Patnaik

All rights reserved. No part of this book may be reproduced in any form by any electronic, mechanical, photocopying, recording means or otherwise, including information storage and retrieval systems, without permission in writing from the publisher, except in the case of brief quotations embodied in critical articles and reviews.

First Edition	: August, 2025
Published by	: Dr. Tanmay Panda & Dr. Sunanda Mishra Panda Vidya Publishing Inc., Toronto, Canada || Bhubaneswar, Odisha
Website	: www.vidyapublishing.com
Email	: vidyapublishinginc@gmail.com
Cell	: +1 6478389884
Odisha Contact	: Nirmalya Garden, Plot 516/1719, House 10, KIIT Post Office, Patia, Bhubaneswar - 751024
Cell	: +91 8984131810
Cover Design	: Harish Chandra Das Printed in India, Biswanath Enterprises
Price	: ₹ 150 /-

Contents

• • • •

1. Into the School Days

What can be gifted to mother this time? She has never desired anything in life.

Her entire life she draped a simple Sambalpuri cotton saree. She accessorized with a chain of beads around her neck. Her radiant beauty had withered away amidst hardship and struggles of youth. The constant demands of her children, the complaints of her husband, and the relentless taunts of her mother-in-law had left her hair streaked with gray.

"Ma, should I dye your hair black this time?" My elder sister asked persistently.

"Will you shut up or you want me to box your ears? You want to dye my gray hair and make me look youthful at this age?" she retorted from the kitchen, irritated.

Ma had no interest in artificial beauty or fashion trends. She saw them as unnecessary distractions.

This vacation, a Sambalpuri handloom saree might make a good gift for her. Yet, she might just say, "What use do I have for these sarees and ornaments now?" She would store it neatly in her wardrobe, occasionally showing it to friends and relatives. They would exclaim, "What a fortunate mother!" And that fleeting pride would fill her heart.

But before even thinking about her saree, Ma would ask if anything was brought for the rest of the family. "Did you bring something for everyone else?" she would ask, as if embarrassed to care about her own needs.

No, such an awkward situation should not arise. Something for Mamun (maternal uncle) would also have to be included. After all, since the sudden demise of their father just before his matriculation examinations, it was Mamun who had shouldered the household responsibilities. His dedication and resilience were unflinching, ensuring the family stayed afloat without falling apart.

It had been eight years since that tragedy, and now, with a stable job in Bangalore, he was coming home to spend the Dussehra holidays in the village. It would be a reunion with childhood friends who had scattered across the country for work, leaving the dusty village school far behind.

It was not just about sarees or shoes—it was about gratitude, love, and the weight of memories borne with silent dignity. He knew this trip home was not just about reunions, but also about recognizing those sacrifices and celebrating the simple pleasures that had shaped his life.

He is coming back home nearly three years after he got this job. He is hoping to celebrate Dussehra in his village this time. His school friends, who work in Surat, Bangalore, Chennai, and Mumbai, will also return home for the holidays. This time, they will all meet during the festival. They had studied together in the village school, which had tin and thatched roofs.

They had completed their education in that dilapidated school, which had no science lab, library, or electricity supply, and had passed with good marks. Since Odisha did not offer them jobs or factories to work in, they had to leave their village and migrate to distant places. During festivals and holidays, they would return home, carrying bundles of gifts and goods.

Ashutosh had found a job in Bangalore, while Amit worked in the textile industry in Surat. Arjun, however, had stayed back in the village. He had heard that Arjun had started a charitable organization providing care, free education, and shelter for orphaned children.

When old friends gather, whether at the Dussehra pandal, the clubhouse, or under the sprawling banyan tree, waves of laughter ripple through their reunion. Tales from their school days are served afresh, wrapped in humour and nostalgia. If Sanskrit teacher "Guruji" or Hrishi Sir arrives there, a friendly competition erupts among the friends to seek his blessings.

"Tell me, how many of you imbibed the noble deeds of your teachers who truly dedicated their life for the pupils? What's the use of this showy devotion?" remarks the Sanskrit Pandit with a smirk.

Yes, the Panditji would surely have to accept some offerings. His true test came fifteen days before exams when his father passed away unexpectedly. In his small three-room mud-baked house, grief-stricken relatives huddled together, overcome with sorrow. Throughout the night, muffled cries filled the air, as someone or another wept inconsolably. His mother, devastated by her husband's death, fainted repeatedly. No one in the house had the mind to check who had eaten or who had gone to bed hungry.

The nextday, the Sanskrit teacher came to the house.

"Ashutosh, my boy," Sir called out. "Come. Take your books and two sets of clothes in your bag and come with me."

"Sir, where are we going?"

"To my house. My son is there too preparing for exams. You will study there. The exam is just thirteen days away. How can you study properly in this noisy environment? You will stay at my house until the exam is over. Come on."

"But Sir..." Ashutosh hesitated.

"I will inform your mother and uncle. You are my responsibility now. Let's go."

That day, if he hadn't left home with Pandit Sir, he wouldn't have been able to take his matriculation exam that year. No one could say how his life's course might have been blocked at that crucial juncture.

Eight years had passed since then.

By the time he reached his village by bus from Bhubaneswar, it was already eleven in the morning. After freshening up, he found his mother had prepared parathas and curry for him.

"Who knows if you ate anything last night? First, have this breakfast. Once your friends arrive, you won't get time to eat. They came looking for you two or three times this morning. Even Pandit Sir's son came asking about you," his mother said.

"What was he saying?"

"Eat first, then we'll talk."

After finishing his meal, Ashutosh opened his trolley bag and pulled out a saree for his mother. She was taken aback.

"Oh my, why did you bring such an expensive saree for me? It's not like I go out anywhere to wear this. Such a heavy silk saree won't suit me! It would look much better on your aunt. She will be delighted," she said, just as his uncle walked in.

"Look at this! Ashutosh has brought a Sambalpuri saree for your wife!" his mother announced.

"Wow! We must acknowledge Ashu's taste. It's wonderful. Now, what did you bring for me?" his uncle asked playfully.

For his uncle, Ashutosh opened a box containing a pair of size-seven leather shoes.

"Oh, come on... don't you know my condition? Ever since my diabetes worsened, my feet have been swelling. No medicine has helped. I can't even wear slippers, let alone shoes. How much did these cost? A thousand? Twelve hundred?"

"Five thousand," Ashutosh replied.

"Why did you spend so much? Never mind... These will fit your cousin Tulu perfectly," his uncle said, picking up the shoes and the saree before stepping outside.

Yet, his face reflected deep joy and satisfaction.

"You all have studied so hard and become fine individuals. Won't God reward your hard work? He definitely will..." his uncle murmured as he walked away barefoot, filled with gratitude.

Just then, his childhood friend Amit arrived. He had become a design engineer at a textile firm in Surat.

"Come on, let's go to Arjun's help school. He has set up a school for orphaned children, providing them with food, shelter, and education. He has gathered twenty-five local kids for his school. Let's go and understand his vision."

Ashutosh tore a leaf from his cheque book and slipped it into his pocket. Holding a gift bag for Pandit Sir, he asked, "How far is Arjun's school? Should we stop by Pandit Sir's house on the way?"

Reaching Pandit Sir's home, Ashutosh bowed and touched his feet. Sir was sitting inside, resting on a wheelchair.

"What's this? Sir can't walk anymore?"

Feeling overwhelmed, Ashutosh pulled out his gift—a sturdy cane made of thick bamboo.

"I brought this for you, Sir," he said, placing the cane in Pandit Sir's hands with reverence.

"Ashutosh, my boy, you took too long to come. It has been a year since I started using this wheelchair. After my knee surgery, I lost the ability to walk. I am a cripple now. I can no longer even stand with the support of a cane."

"Yes, Sir. It has been two years since I last visited the village."

"Alright, give me the cane. It's very beautiful. I asked so many people to get me a sturdy bamboo cane... If possible, place it near the front wall, where the thorny creeper is. Every time I see it, I will remember that my dear student, Ashutosh, brought it for me."

Hearing his teacher's words, Ashutosh's eyes welled up with tears. He returned with a heart heavy with emotions.

Then comes Arjun's help school. A house of mud and bamboo with a thatched roof. Behind the big courtyard, a kitchen with a sloping tin roof. The mud floor, smeared with cow dung, looks clean, with a neatly spread rice-straw mat.

As soon as Amit steps through the school's entrance, children of various ages gather around him and garland him with flowers. Behind them stands Arjun.

Arjun asks the children to sit.

"Twenty-five children are growing up day by day. The space in the house is gradually becoming smaller for them. This house was built on my father's small patch of land. He had left the land for his cattle shed. The school runs with the help of generous people. We are somehow managing the daily needs, but I can't see what lies ahead. From this small rural setup, children have grown up to become great engineers, builders, and doctors of the country. But the helpless village remains the same neglected remote hamlet ...," he added.

Amit extended a cheque of one lakh rupees to Arjun for the school as part of his contribution. The children, filled with joy and gratitude, applauded enthusiastically.

Ashutosh glanced at his own cheque for a moment, then tucked it back into his pocket. No, this wouldn't be of much help for the school. The vast stretch of adjacent land near the school, which he was planning to expand, had been earmarked for a farmhouse. But now, he resolved to put it to a meaningful purpose.

"I had preserved this land near the school for my personal use in the future. Now, I am offering it as my contribution to the school. If a hostel is built here, a hundred students can stay and study. If you wish, the land ownership transfer can be completed by tomorrow," Ashutosh declared.

• • • • •

2. Midnight Connection

Basudev was a man of routine. A retired government officer, he spent his evenings reading books and occasionally scrolling through Facebook. One evening, as he went through his notifications, he noticed a friend request from an unfamiliar name: Supriya Mishra. Curious but cautious, he clicked on her profile.

Supriya's timeline revealed a dignified life. She was a schoolteacher, a woman in her early fifties, with a warm smile captured in profile photos. Her posts were filled with pictures of her school events, family gatherings, and captions reflecting her thoughtful nature. The most notable aspect? She had two grown up children, both married and settled abroad. Her husband, a senior bank manager, occasionally appeared in family photographs, looking content and accomplished.

"Seems like a respectable family," Basudev thought. But why would she want to connect with him? They had no mutual friends.

The question lingered in his mind until curiosity won over caution. He accepted the request and left it at that.

Later that night, as the clock struck twelve, Basudev's phone buzzed. The screen flashed an unknown number. Frowning, he answered.

"Hello?"

"Is it Basudev?" a soft yet slightly nervous voice asked.

"Yes. Who's this?"

"It's Supriya...from Facebook," she said hesitantly.

Surprised, Basudev straightened in his chair. "Oh, hello, Mrs. Mishra. It's rather late—"

"I know, I'm sorry for calling at this hour. I didn't want to disturb you during the day," she interrupted, her voice trembling. "I just thought... we could talk."

"About what, exactly?" he asked, his tone steady but curious.

There was a pause. Then, she said, "About life...and perhaps, about finding someone to talk to. I hope you don't mind."

Her words left him momentarily speechless. What could a woman, seemingly content in her family life, possibly need from him?

Supriya's voice softened again, but this time it carried a hint of insistence. "Mr. Basudev, life is what we make of it, you said. That's a very... pragmatic answer. But tell me, don't you sometimes feel like there's more to life than just... routines and responsibilities?"

Basudev leaned back in his chair, her words pulling at something deep within him. "I suppose I've thought about it now and then," he admitted. "But at my age, one learns to accept life for what it is. Every phase has its own purpose."

"That's true," she said thoughtfully. "But don't you think acceptance sometimes becomes an excuse? A way to avoid asking ourselves if we're truly happy?"

Her question hung in the air, and Basudev felt its weight. "Happiness is a fleeting thing," he replied carefully. "Contentment, however, is something we can choose."

Supriya chuckled lightly, though it was tinged with melancholy. "Contentment. That's such a safe word, isn't it? Tell me, Mr. Basudev, when was the last time you felt truly alive? Not content, but... exhilarated?"

Her words surprised him, and he found himself searching for an answer. He couldn't remember. "I'm not sure I understand your point, Mrs. Mishra. Are you asking if I've missed something in life?"

"Maybe," she said, her voice turning introspective. "Or maybe I'm asking if you've given up on something. You're a man with wisdom and experience. You seem composed, but I wonder... is that composure a mask?"

Basudev felt a flicker of irritation but quickly pushed it aside. "And what about you, Mrs. Mishra?" he countered. "You seem to be probing into my life, but what about your own? Are you asking these questions for me, or for yourself?"

There was a long pause before Supriya answered. "Fair point," she said quietly. "I suppose it's easier to ask questions than to answer them. But to be honest... I've felt invisible for a long time. My family is wonderful, my husband is successful, and my children are settled. Yet, in all of it, I've lost the sense of who I am."

Her confession caught Basudev off guard. He hadn't expected such raw honesty. "That's a difficult feeling," he said after a moment. "But surely there are ways to find yourself again."

"Perhaps," Supriya said. "But it feels like every part of me has been claimed by someone else—my students, my children, my husband. Do you understand what I mean?"

Basudev nodded, though she couldn't see him. "I do. In a way. We all make sacrifices, but sometimes we forget to leave something for ourselves."

"Exactly," she said, her voice brightening slightly. "That's why I reached out to you. I thought... maybe you'd understand."

Her words unsettled him. They hinted at a connection she seemed to be searching for—one he wasn't sure he could or should provide. "Mrs. Mishra, I think it's important to understand the boundaries of this... friendship. I'm willing to listen, but we must be careful not to overstep."

Supriya sighed. "Of course. I appreciate your honesty, Mr. Basudev. I hope you don't think poorly of me for speaking so openly."

"Not at all," he said, though he felt the need to end the conversation soon. "Sometimes, it's good to have someone to talk to. But let's keep things... balanced."

"I understand," she said. "Thank you for listening. And I hope... maybe next time, you'll share a little more about yourself."

Basudev hesitated before replying. "Goodnight, Mrs. Mishra."

"Goodnight," she said softly, and the call ended.

As Basudev set his phone down, he stared at it for a long time. What had he just opened himself up to? And why did he feel like this conversation had pulled at something within him he hadn't realized was there?

Basudev sat silently for a moment, staring at the phone in his hand. Something about the conversation gnawed at him. Supriya's words—her probing questions about his privacy, her openness about her dissatisfaction—seemed oddly calculated, as if she were testing the waters for something beyond mere friendship.

He shook his head, dismissing his unease. "You're overthinking," he muttered to himself. Rising from his chair, he switched off the lights in his study and headed to bed.

Just as he was about to lie down, his phone buzzed again. It was another call from the same unknown number.

Reluctantly, he picked up. "Mrs. Mishra, it's late. What is it now?"

There was silence on the other end. Then a voice—not Supriya's, but a man's—spoke, low and menacing.

"So, Basudev, are you enjoying my wife's attention?"

Basudev's blood ran cold. "Who is this?"

"Who do you think? I'm Supriya's husband," the man growled. "Did you really think you could chat with her behind my back and get away with it?"

Basudev's mind raced. "Listen, I don't know what you're implying, but this is a misunderstanding. Your wife contacted me. I've done nothing wrong."

The man laughed darkly. "Nothing wrong? Accepting her friend request, talking to her late at night, letting her spill her feelings to you? You've already crossed the line, old man."

"I didn't encourage her!" Basudev protested, his voice rising. "She reached out to me. I was only being polite."

"You think politeness will save you? Let me tell you something—Supriya isn't what she seems. And now that you've entertained her, you're part of her game."

"Game?" Basudev repeated, his throat dry.

"She does this," the man continued. "Reaches out to men, plays the helpless woman, and when they get too close... she destroys them. You're her latest target."

Basudev felt his knees weaken. "I don't believe you. She sounded... genuine."

The man's voice dropped to a whisper, sending chills down Basudev's spine. "That's her skill. She's a predator, and you're her prey. Don't say I didn't warn you."

The line went dead. Basudev stood frozen, the phone still in his hand. His mind reeled with questions. Who was telling the truth? Was Supriya really a manipulative schemer? Or was her husband trying to control her, using threats to keep her isolated?

As he sank into his chair, the phone buzzed again. This time, it was a message—from Supriya.

"I'm sorry for involving you in this, Basudev. But you'll soon see why I had to. Don't trust anyone—not even me. Goodnight."

The room seemed to close in around him as he read the message. A cold sweat broke out on his forehead. He realized he had unwittingly become part of something far darker than he could have imagined.

In the silence of the night, a new question took hold: Had Supriya been seeking a confidant—or a pawn in her own dangerous game?

•••

3. Smritirekha

• What have you hidden inside the tin trunk, honey?

"Nothing. Just some memories," Smriti responded.

"Memories are jotted down in diaries. Who hides them in a trunk?" Anurag asked, puzzled.

"Where else would I keep them if not in a trunk? Or in a closet?"

"Things you want to remember are in your mind already," Smriti smiled in response to Anurag's comment. "And anyone might see the mementoes in the closet. It's a museum anyway," he added.

Anurag lifted the trunk's lid, revealing old photographs and letters. He picked up a photograph, faded but evocative—capturing their wedding forty years ago under a flowering Gulmohar tree. The faces in the photo were all gone now, except the two of them. It was their life's first thrill—joy and tears apparent on their faces.

Their first encounter had been at a poetry reading festival, a dream shared. Despite resistance from conservative families, they had signed the marriage contract in front of the registrar. In the years that followed, they welcomed their children.

Their eldest daughter was witness to State Writers Confab hosted in their hometown. It was attended by the then

Chief Minister among other renowned writers of the time. Smriti still remembered the host of authors who visited their home. One author had nicknamed Smriti as "Golden Bhabi," though she couldn't recall the name anymore.

Memories had faded over time. She had been diagnosed with Dementia, and slowly, inevitably, the disease began to degenerate her memory cells behind thalmus bone. She could no longer remember dates, faces, places, events— and sometimes even the people closest to her.

One evening, sitting beside her on a bench in a nearby park, Anurag gently held her hand. "Let's go for a drive," he suggested.

"Where should we go?" she asked, a slight glimmer in her eye.

"To your village," he said, smiling warmly. "To your home Dhuaan-Dhar near Bhanjanagar town." Smriti was excited to learn about the destination. "Oh, it's my home. How I miss it so much," she exclaimed.

As they drove, Anurag talked of the river Rusikulya, in Ganjam district of Odisha.

She listened, intrigued but with a distant look in her eyes. They passed the fields, the roads winding through landscapes familiar yet foreign to her.

"We used to leap into the water as children daily. There used to be a banyan tree on the bank. Rushikulya was in spate," Smriti recounted. The river turns ferocious and cruel in the rainy season.

"Are we really going to my village?" she asked again, a trace of excitement conspicuous in her voice.

"Yes, to your childhood home by the banks of the river Rushikulya."

She looked out of the window, her face reflected a mixture of joy and wonder. For a moment, Smriti seemed like her old self — hopeful, alive, jovial and impressed.

"Our village lies by the banks of the Rushikulya River. Holding onto the banyan tree roots by the embankment, we would dive into the river. When tired, we would swim back to the shore."

Nonsense. Who can swim against the swollen currents in the rainy season?

I didn't say it was the rainy season. Smrutirekha objected. Is it the rainy season now? This is winter.

Can you swim in the river in winter? The water would be as cold as ice!

"Though it's cold outside, the water feels warm once you're inside the river. You wouldn't know", Smrutirekha said. Really? You can bathe in cold water?

"Yes. If we have a cold, mother forbids us from going to the river. She heats water at home and bathes us herself."

Do you feel like bathing in the river now? Let's try. Jump in then, said Anurag.

No, not now. Let's go home first. Let's see mother. Then we can talk. Onward to our home...

Parking the car, Anurag walked with Smriti toward the house. Seeing strangers in the home, Smrutirekha asked them about her mother. They didn't understand her question. How could they tell her about someone who had passed away twenty years ago, blending into the elements?

Ignoring them, Smrutirekha moved toward the backyard. She looked around in wonder at the garden, the well, and the cow shed. There was no cow shed; there was a brick-walled kitchen. The well was covered with a new metal lid. The moss on the back wall of the well was scraped off.

Perhaps this time, memories from childhood will help Smrutirekha remember the truth. If her childhood memories come back, she might be able to accept reality in its present form.

Wasn't there a drumstick tree here? She kept asking. Where did the tree go?

The tree must have aged and died, she said, though she still couldn't believe it.

How could the tree have died? Why didn't I know about it? Smrutirekha repeated her distress.

Mother used to cook here for you. She used to braid your hair. After eating food cooked by mother, you would go to the school. She's no longer here; she has passed away. It's been twenty years. She loved you so much – you wouldn't believe it.

Holding her hand, Anurag led her out of the house. In front lay the fog-covered village deity. Behind her was the riverbank where Smrutirekha's mother's final rites were performed.

After our marriage, we came here for the first time. You

drew water from the backyard well and poured it over my feet. We climbed up the steps nearby. Do you remember?

Smrutirekha couldn't recall anything. She couldn't even believe what Anurag was saying. She couldn't accept that her mother had been cremated at this burial ground.

Who are you? How do you know my mother? Where is my mother? I'll go to her... Smrutirekha insisted.

Anurag felt an unfamiliar sadness weigh on his chest. Smrutirekha couldn't recognize him even though they had shared a life for many years!

"Don't you recognize me, Smruti? We've spent forty years together as husband and wife. I'm Anurag... we have three children. Our home is in Bhubaneswar. We married for love. Don't you remember?"

"You're lying. You're a liar. Who are you to marry me? I'm not married to you. I don't know you at all. I need my mother..." Smrutirekha said, breaking free of Anurag's grip.

Anurag didn't know what to do. His eyes grew moist as he looked up in despair. Would he ever get Smruti back? Or was she lost forever, buried in the depths of oblivion?

• • • •

4. Fawn and the Prince

Nandan stepped out of the mansion. He was just five. Heard repeated hammering in the woods. Who is doing this amidst tranquility? He couldn't stay tuned in to the mellifluous vibration emanating from nearby Paradise.

Is this a noisy bird or a fairy beating drums?

He stepped on the carpet of grass surrounding yellow and crimson flowers. He rolled down like a sledgehammer on snow.

What's on the flipside of the meadows?

Nandan stepped. There was a rustle through the leaves. Is this the wind playing flute with boughs of sander?

Nandan called the approaching fawn, "Hi ... hold on..." The animal heard the child. It paused for a moment.

"Who is this? Come on, come on ... how can I help you?"

"What exists beyond that hill? I wanna watch who is tapping on a trunk."

"No, it's a woodpecker. Its coloured wings have a sense of proportion. It drills holes into the tree. That's Nature's testimony, I know."

Why? The five-year-old's anxiety grows.

"The woodpecker knows its prey's hiding place underneath the bark. It picks insects holed up in trees with its sticky tongue. Its legs are short, firm," said the deer.

"Do insects taste sweet?" He asked.

The woodpecker savours worms. They are as sweet as raisins," responds the animal.

"Sweet berries? You know where do we pluck berries from? I like plums. I wanna eat them."

"All right, let's go ahead and eat those purple-black plums. Then we'll meet the woodpecker."

Duo sensed the fragrance of sandalwood in the forest. After a short walk, the fawn stands under a tree.

"Hey, what's this place? How far is the vine?"

"Look, look up. Watch those cluster of berries...red, purple and ripe fruits," points out the quadruped.

"How do I pluck fruits? I'm short, I can't get my hands on it", said Nandan.

"Of course, you will eat the plums if you wish. Depends on your spiritual strength".

"What's Spiritual?"

"It's a soul's wish seeking fulfilment. You can savour fruits if you wish firmly..."

"What about you? Won't you like some fruits?"

"I'll have grass from our farmland. Please, pick your raisins. Raise your hands at the fruit.The tree will bow down to your height", says the deer.

Nandan raises his hands. A large bough bends down. A bunch of black berries swings near Nandan while the deer picks up leaves from syzygium cumini branch.

"Oh, how sweet the leaves are!"

"Do leaves taste sweat?"

"No. Pick the hanging plums. Delicious and succulent. Leave the leaves for me, focus on fruits."

What's this berry's name?

"Jambolanum. Black plums. This comes from our ancestors domiciled in Jambudweep that's Bharat. Eat them to your heart's content. But don't overeat. If you submit to gula or gluttony, you'll lose your peace".

"It's so peaceful... tranquil here, I enjoy this."

"Do you see? Nothing wrong with hunger but greed is dangerous. There are no takers for jamuns here. The fragrance of spring chills the wind. There is no dust, or humidity. There is moisture in the soil. The Sun is soothing, but it doesn't freeze the earth after dusk. This climate depends on our psychic state."

"Let's get back home. The sun is rolling down in the West. Everyone in the royal clan may be waiting for us," says Nandan. ... But I can't go home now. I am thirsty, get me something to sip," he appeals.

"Come on then. If we reach the valley beyond that hill, we can access clear and clean water. Enough cool water to drink. Come on, let's go down then," the fawn leads the way to the stream. Its other end has a hoard of jumbos playing water sport with their calves.

"Lo, on the other bank has a group of tigers. An invisible fence separates elephants from the tigers in the sanctuary."

The angelic child enters the stream along with the fawn. Very soft water! They rejoice.

The boundaries of the wild, mild and sober animals are predetermined. Everyone is confined to their territories. How beautiful is the animal world! He exclaims.

Nature's elements are tranquil and lovely in this part: Trees, humans, birds, animals and fairies are in their best poetic order. Rulers of this era are Shri Janardhan and Srilakshmi. They are none other than his parents! Nine lakh subjects of this kingdom are happy, thanks to their wealth and bliss. We're people of divine origin. Parents are guardians of honesty, religion and justice. We can't think of war, anger, lust, sickness or violence in this Heaven.

Nandan pats the deer's back after drinking water. They walk a few more steps. "If you get tired, you can fly back home. Don't worry."

"How? Where is the flying cart?" Nandan wanted to know.

"Aren't we going to the woodpecker? The flying machine can be seen right under the tree the woodpecker perches on."

The bird watched the deer following the child. The conversation between boy and the fawn silenced the bird atop the tree.

"Strangers? Who are they? " The woodpecker whispers in apprehension.

"Nandan is here to visit you. He is gentle and sweet."

"Quis es? Who are you at this hour?"

"I am a deer cub. We inhabit River Saraswati valley pastor land. By temperament I'm cool."

"It means you too are an ascetic creature. But I'm a poor bird. I drill holes into live trees. I am glad you've come to visit us. It's dark, I can't see you now because of poor visibility. I'll be happy to meet you tomorrow morning. Good night," the bird said.

Nandan and the fawn bid adieu to the bird and approach the flower-bedecked flying cart.

"Please take your seat. Recite swaman, a hymn from occult book. You can reach your mansion. This is Tantric science. There are mechanical gears too. Watch the pedals under your seat. Press the right pedal to go down, and left to go up. The middle one is accelerator to move forward. There's a right handle to turn cart right and a left handle to move left. That's how it works. Come on," commanded the fawn.

The child returns to his palace along with the fawn. Deities at the mansion heave a sigh of relief from anxiety when they see Nandan.

Is this journey a reality or vision?

"It's the virtual reality of India today."

As the History unveils, the earth was reduced to ashes after World War III and nuclear holocaust. A fresh creation — Epoch of Truth— was imperative after missile wars. The new age of deities christened Satyuga begins in 2030 at the culmination of imperialism, terrorism and ailments caused by viruses hitherto unheard of."

How do people live now?

"People? Everyone here is a spirit conscious angel. Love and humanism are basic tenets of the new world order.

Happiness, love, peace, wisdom, purity and power are inherent attributes of individuals."

Greed for food, gold and possessions are expelled by intensive penance and renunciation. Knowledge and practice of Yoga burn lust and attachment here. And India comprising deities will integrate spiritualism and good governance!

Well, back to the monarchical regime? None knows.

• • • •

5. A Stormy Night

Who knocks at the door in the dead of night during a storm? Who dares enter the chamber of a lonely young man? It's a woman in the rain?

The rain poured relentlessly, drumming against the earth with increasing intensity. Amidst the downpour, a sudden knock echoed against the door.

Who could it be at such an hour? And who was knocking? Shashank couldn't make sense of it.

He wasn't sure what time it was. Then, in a sudden flash of lightning, he noticed his phone plugged into the charging board. Checking it, he saw it was nearly two in the morning. Darkness engulfed the room—the electricity had gone out at some point. It wasn't easy in the city's dark alleys to guess when the power supply might be restored.

A faint voice called out his name from the other side of the door.

"Shashank... Shashank Babu, will you please listen for a moment?"

"Who? Who's there?"

"It's me, Annie ... Anyone in?"

Who is it at this unearthly hour? Noise of wings flapping on his door was audible.

Panicked residents of low-lying areas of the Bay had no clues left about where the storm will landfall. Met centres had warned of impending danger to the Indian coast and Bangladesh which always is a certain victim of storm. It's too early to hazard a guess about the storm's ferocity.

The wall clock struck two. Someone is reciting his name, Sashank, Sashank. Will you please open the door?

: Who is it?

I'm Annie, yes, Annie."

: Annie? Who's Annie? He thrust out of the window.

Couldn't make out who it is. For sure. Nothing was visible in the dark.

Please open the door Sashank.

"Who is it?" He opened the door with hesitation. And asked: "Where are you coming from so late? How can

I help you?"

Annie came in with her rain soaked clothes. She was drenched thoroughly.

"I am Annie, the landlord's daughter.... Yes I got wet in the lane from my house before I got in here," she said.

"I've never seen you before. Where did you alight from? What's the matter now? What about your parents? Did I see you earlier? I think no.

"I came from Nagpur in the morning. My parents have left for our country farmhouse. At night. They drove to the village to see our ailing aunty. So I was all alone at home."

: I see. So, what's now? I asked.

"I'm very scared of thunders. Lightnings are frightening. So, I left home as I can't stand loneliness, especially when it's raining. "

Annie was a woman of medium height. She was of wheatish complexion. She'll be about thirty-three years or so.

: Are you married? Where is your husband? And when are you expecting your parents to come back home?

My husband lives in Canada. Comes once a year. My parents? They'll be right back tomorrow.

: You've kids? He asked and then bit his tongue. He shouldn't have asked such personal questions to strangers at such odd hours. He pulled himself up.

: No, I do not have children. I am employed with Koch,

a software company at Nagpur.

: Sit down. You are wet. Wipe it off a bit, he said.

The wind whistled along with gusts outside. The meteorological department had predicted heavy rains as cyclone Phani crosses Odisha coast and heads towards northeastern bay. So you can count on its impact next 24 hours.

: Would you mind a little coffee? He asked.

No, why take trouble at this hour? Said Annie.

He found a candle on the table. Went to gas stove. Lighted it.

The candle was flickering with each whistling wind

pushing through the windows.

: The wind will blow it up, Annie said before shutting the door.

Coffee? He suggested.

No, just a little milk instead will do. You have some milk? She asked Shasank in reciprocation.

"Yes. I too love coffee," He said as she warmed up the milk.

What's your blood pressure count?

: Why? Mine is 120-190 at bedtime and 45-140 at breakfast.

I know. It isn't good, she said.

Isn't good for what? Blood pressure?

Coffee pumps blood pressure up, said Annie picking

up milk from his hands.

When is your wife reaching home?

"She is one of the reasons that shoot up my blood pressure. Workplace pressures and mobile phones usually raise pressures. Coffee isn't the culprit alone. My wife will be back after vacations," he responded.

Annie leaned slightly on the couch holding the milk. How long should we spend in the dark like this? She mumbled.

Who knows how many boughs might have broken down on the power cables during the storm.

Honestly, your baby is so cute ... Sashask was shocked to hear Annie's compliments.

Have you ever seen our child? He asked.

"Yes, I saw this photo on your table a while ago," replied Annie.

Shashank felt relieved, though the sight of the candle lamp swaying in the wind once again filled him with doubt.

"Alright then, your fear should have gone now. The rain will last all night. Maybe you can go home alone now," said Shashank, opening the door.

"No, let me stay a little longer. I can't go back alone now. Please," Annie pleaded.

Shashank's eyes, heavy with drowsiness, began to burn. Outside, the storm was raging. As he debated what to do, the candle wick flapped wildly in the gusty wind and vanished into the darkness.

The rain-soaked night devoured Shashank's entire being. The wind howled, mingling with the relentless drumming of the rain. Slowly, his weary eyes closed.

The rain subsided a little towards dawn.

When he woke up, the sky was overcast. In the dim morning fog, he remembered Annie. That night, she had come to him with her drenched, trembling body. What did she want? He hadn't understood.

He got up and looked around—no one was on the sofa. But beneath it, his vest and shirt lay crumpled. Shashank searched the house. No one was there, except himself.

Stepping outside, he saw the landlord.

"When did you return from the village?" he asked.

"We never left for the village. Who told you so?" the landlord replied.

"Annie told me. She said her uncle was unwell..." Shashank said hesitantly.

"Annie? Who's Annie?" the landlord asked.

"Your daughter. She arrived from Nagpur last night," Shashank clarified.

"We don't have a daughter with that name. Who had come from Nagpur?" The landlord looked perplexed.

"If not Annie who else knocked on my door last night? She claimed to be your daughter. She said her husband lives in Canada," Shashank explained.

"Who knows what creature came — perhaps a night wanderer, a bulbul, or a storm spirit," the landlord muttered as he walked away.

"A night wanderer? What do you mean?" Shashank called after him.

"You don't know? It was probably a nocturnal being called Succubus — a spirit that visits lonely men at night, wakes them from their sleep, and satisfies its own desires."

"A Succubus? Are those real?"

"Yes, a petini... a lustful spirit that ensnares men, strips them bare while they sleep," the landlord said, his voice fading as he walked off into the mist.

• • • •

6. Mom in Retrospect

Suddenly, someone's sobbing woke me up.

Father was lying on the bed next to mine, his face buried in the pillow, crying like a child.

I had never seen my father cry before, though I had cried many times in childhood because of his scoldings.

From the inner courtyard, a faint scent of incense wafted into the room.

Not long ago, Mother had been with us. Her presence had been regal. She wore a freshly washed cotton saree, perfect for the damp winter. When anyone approached her, she would first gesture toward the wooden bench, inviting them to sit, and then ask, "Have you eaten?"

Today, she had left us all behind. The news had already been conveyed to my brothers living outside Odisha over the phone. When she passed away, no one was by her side. Reaching Capital Bhubaneswar in time was impossible for anyone.

Everything had been normal that morning. After breakfast, she had sat down with an old book of Bhagwat Gita and eventually dozed off. She woke up around two in the afternoon.

She had just taken a few bites of food when, suddenly, she gasped for breath. She coughed once, then fell silent. Her eyes remained open, staring blankly. She stayed exactly where she was — on the woven mat beside her plate of rice.

Now, I was lying on the same cot where she had breathed her last. I glanced at the clock — it was 2:30 AM.

Mother's body lay still on a wooden bier in the courtyard. Cotton plugs had been placed in her nostrils and ears. Near her head, an oil lamp flickered in the dim glow of the funeral lamps.

My sister-in-law, instead of sitting beside the body, had fallen asleep nearby. My niece, Jhilli, had curled up against her shoulder. My wife, too, had dozed off beside them.

Mother had no illness, no lingering ailments of any order — except the death itself.

The mother of four sons, now eighty-eight years old, had grown skeletal from a lifetime of fasting and religious observances. Her frail body lay stretched on the wooden cot, lifeless. Silent now. Otherwise, she was always murmuring, whispering to herself.

Father worked in the jail department. His days were spent in the office, leaving him with no time to play with us or chat. We never expected him to be present on our birthdays, parties, or festivals. Our childhood was spent mostly in our mother's company.

I must have been four or five years old. One day, before leaving for the office, I told him, "Papa, bring me a police cap."

It was a dry, scorching day. After eating, I sat in the courtyard, waiting for my father to return. He usually walked back from the jail around two in the afternoon. I watched from the porch as he approached – his hands empty, no police cap.

Had he forgotten such a small thing? Disappointed, I ran towards him and cried out, "Why, Papa? Where's my cap?"

"Oh... I forgot dear. I'll definitely bring it tomorrow," he replied.

But I was stubborn. "No! I need it now! I can't wait until tomorrow."

He sighed. "The shop must be closed by now. I'll bring it in the evening."

I argued, "By the time you return from the office, it will be night. The shop'd be shut then. I want it now."

Father tried to refuse, but I was so adamant that he had no choice. He turned around and walked back toward the market. I ran after him, barefoot. Seeing my determination, he scooped me up in his arms and took me along.

We went to Fakir's stationary shop near our house, where he bought me a small hat. As soon as I placed it on my head, I felt content like a jailor. I ran home and showed it to my mother. Only after she inspected it did I finally calm down.

From that day on, I never nagged my father for toys or books.

As I grew older, she never let me sit alone in the courtyard. Every afternoon, after lunch, she would call me while reading her Sriptures. Among her favorite books was the **Shrimad Bhagvad Gita**.

Whenever I got distracted at the end of a verse, she would patiently explain it to me in simple Odia, my mother-tongue.

Lord Krishna advises Arjuna in **Bhagvad Gita**:

"Those with limited intellect worship minor deities and idols of wood and stone. After death, they take birth as spirits or in the wilderness. But those who recognize my true nature and worship me reach my divine abode, Vaikuntha."

I asked, "Then what about the wooden deities we worship in temples? Does that mean we, too, have limited intellect?"

"There is no doubt about it," she replied. Scriptures cannot go wrong. "We lack a proper understanding of God. He is formless, infinite divine essence, yet we worship Him in various forms, placing Him in temples. Doesn't that make us narrow-minded?"

"But you said Krishna is God," I countered.

"The Gita says that God is **Ajonijanma** unborn—without birth. Yet, we celebrate Krishna's birth on Janmashtami, believing he was born in Mathura. He also died, struck by an arrow from the tribal hunter Jara," my mother explained clearly.

"So then, who is God, and where is He?" I asked instinctively.

Mother said, "He is formless, without a physical shape. But we know Krishna had a dark-complexioned body, so how can we call him the formless God when he is a human being?"

"Then who is formless?" I asked again.

She read from the Gita: "God exists in everything—as the Supreme Brahman, within wood and stone, in fire and the sky..."

I innocently asked, "If God is everywhere, why do we seek Him or go to temples?"

Mom agreed with my question. "That is exactly why we are called people of limited intellect. If we truly understand that He is formless, then why seek Him here and there?"

"But Mom, if God has no form, why do we worship Goddess Durga with ten arms and ten weapons?"

"You fool," she said. "The artisans who sculpt Durga idols—have they ever actually seen the real Goddess Durga? If the idol were truly divine, why do we submerge it in water after worship? That is blind faith."

Despite her limited formal education, my mother explained me that humans become divine through their virtues—like Krishna and Rama did so. Likewise, through vices, one can become a demon, like Ravana or Mahishasura or Kamsa. But God is an unseen force, not something carved into images or sculpted from wood and stone for worship.

But the priests and pujharis in temples perform rituals, don't they?" I asked.

"Oh, my child, what do priests truly know about God? Can reciting mantras and verses make a stone idol divine? Have you ever seen people offering flowers to Gandhi or Buddha's statue now that they are gone?"

"Then what does it all mean?"

Mother explained, "If God is the Supreme Soul, then we are individual souls because we are His children. The

Supreme Soul and the soul in particular never die—only the physical body dies. He understands all our desires and needs. Nothing is hidden from the Supreme Father.

"Just like a normal father He fulfills all the needs of His children. See how your papa writes down in a list before going to the market—he remembers everything and ensures our wants are met."

"But what does God want from us?" I asked.

"He wants us to be like Him—bodiless, free from sorrow, worries, desires and the fear of death. He tells us to detach from all worldly desires, just as He is. Because we are not merely physical beings—when the body perishes, we become like celestial beings. That is why the Gita says, **Man-mana bhava**—immerse your mind in Me. Come, let us free ourselves from worldly attachments and journey to the realm of divine souls."

Suddenly, the door bell rang.

Father got up from his chair, wiped his face, and asked, "Have the guests arrived?"

I said, "No."

"Has the priest come? Has the canopy been set up? Go, arrange fifty or sixty chairs. Relatives will be arriving. Place your mother's large photo in the courtyard."

I simply nodded and stepped outside. The sky was clearing up.

Mother lay in the courtyard.

A deep silence filled the house.

Beside her, the lamp on the altar burned steadily—like an ascetic soul, unwavering, as if for eternity.

• • • •

7. Choice of a Bride

You have fallen in love with an unknown girl at first sight. What could her name be?

You both have been sitting across from each other for ten minutes. That's it. No words exchanged... A rectangular table separates you. A cup of coffee rests on the table. Both of you are waiting for another cup.

When the waiter arrives, another coffee will be ordered. But it hasn't been ordered yet! If merely looking at someone leads to admiration, is that love? Need not be. It may be physical attraction. Infatuation. Again and again, her eyes, nose, brows, forehead, and lips captivate you. Her black hair is tied with a white clip. Large rings, either silver or plastic, dangle from her ears. Don't they seem a little too big for her ears? Below the rings, a small green stone glistens.

You don't know her name, but you wish to. Her face is like a marvelous painting. Her nose, slightly upturned, resembles a tiny black full stop. Her name should be Kangana. What do you expect from her? Nothing. Because when you truly love someone, there are no expectations.

The coffee is getting cold. "You go ahead," you say, extending the coffee cup towards her.

"It's for you Sir. I don't drink coffee," she says, pushing the cup back toward you. The elderly woman sitting beside her also says, "You have it my son. Jhilli doesn't drink tea or coffee."

Oh! So her name is Jhilli. Now you know. Another beautiful girl sits to the right of the elderly woman. If she is your elder brother's choice, she will be your sister-in-law. You won't look at her with desirous eyes. Criminal eyes are the most dangerous. They can mislead even unknown women, like a hypnotic spell.

Meanwhile, Jhilli steals a couple of glances at you. But she doesn't speak.

You also remain silent, as if you have no role in this situation. Or as if there's nothing you can do.

Looking at it another way, you are the true hero of this drama, the protagonist of this story. This play revolves around you. The scene includes your mother, your brother, a prospective sister-in-law, and her mother. Sitting to her left is a cute younger girl whom you silently interpret in your mind. But why are you looking at her? Have you fallen for her? Or are you searching for the right moment to express your love? You are lost in these thoughts.

"What do you plan to do after your post-graduation?" your brother asks. No one answers.

"Jharnâ, answer him," her mother prompts her. "Will you study after PG?"

"I don't know... If I get a Ph.D. seat, I'll do research," says Jharnâ.

"If you get a research seat, will you study for three more years?"

"Don't take her words seriously. If her in-law's family permits, she may study. If not, she won't," her mother interjects.

Your brother eats dosa, Jharnâ and her mother drink coffee. You finish your coffee in a single gulp.

"Was your coffee cold?" Jhilli's mother asks. A meaningful smile spreads across Jhilli's lips.

Then, your brother, Jharnâ, and her mother continue their discussion about family, household matters, and cooking.

How much have you studied?

How much has she studied?

How much property do you have?

How much do we have?

You and Jhilli exchange glances now and then, followed by subtle smiles. You know this isn't proper behaviour at a first meeting. If someone wished, they could sue you for breaching moral conduct.

How is this a violation? You might ask.

Under Section 354(B) of the Indian Penal Code, if a man exchanges indecent looks against a woman's will, it is considered an obscene gesture. If she feels offended, she can file a police complaint. You could easily end up in jail for three years. A lenient judge might even impose a fine.

"Any job plans?" Your brother asks again.

"I haven't thought about it," Jharnâ replies.

"Any more questions left?" your mother asks your elder brother. "Exchange phone numbers. We can continue discussions over the phone later."

But what are you thinking?

Will our brother accept Jharnâ as a bride? If they get engaged, will your path become easier?

Nothing is certain in life. Maybe you have started to realize that life is like an unexpected storm. It gives no prior warning. And yet, one must always be prepared — for storms, rain, winters, and springs.

It's time to leave. Amidst the echoes of collective well-wishes from new acquaintances, you stand there, uncertain. Will you immerse yourself in their blessings and affections? Or will you step out of the hotel and forget everything?

Can you let go of Jhilli's hand and the folds of her dupatta that have unknowingly tied a knot around your heart?

There is chaos in the background, yet you remain still within yourself. Jhilli's gaze and the scent of her body have mesmerized you many times. You cannot wipe them away from the depths of your consciousness. You cannot let go of her hands and the edge of her veil, which have delicately wrapped around the fragile nerves of your mind.

Everyone stood up, gathering their favorite belongings — vanity bags, mobile phones, car and house keys.

"Did you take all the phone numbers?" Jhilli's mother reminded.

Reluctantly, you pressed the keys, saving Jhilli's mobile number. You wondered — would Jhilli ever call you of her own accord?

Before leaving, you encountered Jhilli's secretive glance once more. Hidden from the eyes of others, she offered a subtle smile. That smile has trapped you in uncertainty. Can you trust it and move forward? Or is it merely an illusion of your mind? Should you have asked Jhilli something openly? If you had, the silence surrounding you would have been shattered. But no—the moment slipped away. You walked toward your car, and by then, something already felt forgotten.

Life is perhaps a composition of countless missed chances. At times, you have struck a long stride in frustration, and at others, you have let things go, believing them to be inevitable. But today, knowingly, you ignored the opportunity before you.

"Bye, bye, see you..." you said.

Jhilli waved courteously. Once she was gone, you sat inside the car for a while. In the rearview mirror, you watched as she disappeared into the city's bustling crowd with her family.

Conflict brews within your heart, while excitement stirs all around the city, unsettling you. Is all reality in life so uncertain and full of possibilities? Or, before long, will you meet her again at another café table? And will the veil of silence be lifted forever?

You drove away, leaving the place behind—away from the crowd, into solitude. By evening, you had already forgotten the possibilities you had glimpsed in the morning.

"Did you like the girl or not?" your mother asked your elder brother. Your father looked eager for the answer. Even you felt anxious.

Your elder brother remained silent for a moment.

"What are you thinking so much about? Just say yes or no!"

"Well, there's a little problem," he finally replied.

"What problem?" mother asked. But you sensed something unexpected was coming.

"Talk to her parents first. What if Jhilli, Jharnâ's younger sister, is considered as a bridge instead?" your elder brother suggested.

"What nonsense is this?" your mother exclaimed. "You went to see the elder sister, and now you're asking for the younger one's hand? That's not how things work! Is life some kind of marketplace transaction? No. If you're not interested, just say no from the start! No need for such complications!"

8. All Pervasive Godfather

Papa, what does 'omnipresent' mean? asked ten-year-old Utkarsh. His father was sitting in the courtyard, enjoying the touch of the cool evening breeze. Utkarsh tugged at his father's sleeve, trying to get his attention.

Anand Mohan lifted his face from the newspaper and asked, "What happened now? Who said that? Where did you see the word 'omnipresent'?"

"Papa, today my class teacher said God is everywhere, just like the wind is —omnipresent. But how can God be omnipresent?"

Folding the newspaper, Anand chuckled. "Ah, so God is omnipresent. Fine. Many religions believe this. But do you know? In the Old Testament of the Bible, it is written that God called upon the Sun and the Moon and commanded them to keep moving around the earth, lighting it up. People believed this idea for fifteen hundred years. But later, with the advancement of science, this belief was proven entirely wrong."

Utkarsh frowned in thought. "Yes, Father, I know. The earth moves around the Sun. But..." He hesitated for a moment. "Can the earth move around God?"

Anand leaned forward slightly. "Just as people had a completely wrong idea about the solar system, how can they be sure that their understanding of God is correct? The belief that God is omnipresent doesn't seem right at all. What do you think? Without knowing whether God is bigger or smaller than the earth, how can we claim He is everywhere?"

Utkarsh lowered his head, absorbing his father's words in his young mind. "But Father, if God is everywhere, then He must know about our suffering. People chant hymns and prayers day and night, crying out to Him. Why doesn't He come to help them?"

Anand's expression softened. "Yes, that's exactly the question. If God is everywhere, He must hear people's cries, the hunger in Ethiopia, the poverty in Pakistan. If He knows our troubles, why doesn't He help us?"

Utkarsh looked at his father, troubled. Doubt crept into his mind. "So, it's clear that God does not help those in distress."

Taking a deep breath, Anand gazed westward, where the Sun was disappearing behind the trees. "It's not that simple. I'm not saying God doesn't exist, but I do think we don't have the right understanding of His presence. Look, if we say He is on earth, then why does He have to take incarnations or avatars repeatedly? We know of Vishnu, Shri Ram, Parashuram, Vamana, and Shri Krishna as His incarnations. If God takes human form from time to time, how can He be omnipresent?"

Utkarsh suddenly recalled a story his grandmother had told him. "Right! Grandma said that whenever people are in deep distress, God is born as Rama or Krishna to save them."

Anand nodded in agreement. "Yes, our Scriptures say that God does not always stay in the mortal world. When the burden of sin increases on Earth, He descends to subdue the wicked and protect the virtuous. That's what is written in the Bhagavad Gita."

"Then where is He?" Utkarsh asked in frustration. "If He is not always here, then where does He stay normally?"

Anand smiled, though his gaze remained fixed on the horizon. "That is a mystery. We know He is formless. Perhaps He exists in a way we cannot even imagine. Or maybe He is waiting for us to seek Him out…"

"But how can we find Him? If we don't know where He is or what He is like, how do we search for Him?" Utkarsh repeated, a deep furrow forming on his small forehead. "And are we even capable of finding Him? Are we gods ourselves?"

"No, no," Anand said. "But tell me, when people face suffering, disease, or poverty, what do they do first? Do they call upon God, or seek help from others?"

"They ask their parents, friends, or neighbors for help," Utkarsh replied, as if he were slowly beginning to grasp the essence of human helplessness.

"Yes, that's right," said Anand, his voice carrying a hint of concern. "When someone helps us in difficult times, gives us courage, or expresses sympathy, what do we think? We say that God appeared in that form to show us the way. Isn't that so?"

Utkarsh's mind began to process this. "So, does that mean whenever someone helps us, we can think of God as being present in that moment?"

Anand nodded in agreement. "In a way, yes. The form in which we imagine God may not exist in reality. But the actions we take to help others might be inspired by a hidden divine presence. When we show compassion for someone's suffering or support someone truthfully, a part of God works through us. In that way, divine power manifests in the world — without us even realizing it. Don't you think so?"

"But if we pray in times of need, does He really hear our pleas?" Utkarsh asked in a softer voice.

Anand smiled. "Whether He listens or not, the act of praying first strengthens our inner resolve. It sharpens our vision, focuses our mind, and clarifies our hope. But whether God is somewhere sitting and listening to us, that I cannot say."

"We must still strive for what we truly desire from the depths of our hearts, no matter the obstacles," Anand added.

Utkarsh fell silent for a while. His young mind gradually gathered his scattered thoughts. As the evening light faded, stars began to twinkle in the sky. He looked upward, lost in thought, as if the countless unresolved questions in his mind were shimmering, hidden in the vast darkness of space.

"Father," he said after a moment, his gaze fixed on the constellation of stars. "Do you think God really exists far above the sky, playing hide and seek with the stars?"

Anand also looked up. A blend of joy and melancholy flickered across his face. "Some believe He is above, in a supreme realm where even the light of the Sun, Moon, and stars cannot reach. Others believe God exists in virtues or qualities—love, purity, generosity, compassion, and kindness, present within all of us. But the truth is, no one really knows for sure. For thousands of years, sages and scholars have searched for the answer. Saints and religious leaders have come and gone, yet no one has been able to define God's presence with certainty or discover His true identity."

Utkarsh turned back to his father with curiosity. "Father, if no one knows God, then how do they believe in Him?"

"That is the mystery of faith," Anand replied. "You have never seen Him, yet you believe He exists. That is faith. The belief that there is someone greater than us—stronger, wiser, and more loving—who will rescue us in times of extreme distress, even though we know nothing about Him."

Utkarsh fell silent again. His father's words played in his innocent young mind, leaving a trace of deep thought on his face. Then, as if understanding something, he smiled slightly and said, "But I think God might be present in all good things—truthfulness, service, charity, and kindness..."

Anand gently ran his fingers through his son's unruly hair and said, "You're right. You've understood well. Do you know how the Bible describes Him? As the radiant light of a glorious kingdom. The Creator of heaven and earth, full of love and mercy. A day will come when everyone will worship Him in spirit."

"And what does the Quran say about Him, Father?"

"The Quran describes Allah, or the Supreme Being, as the source of light in heaven and earth — granting humans knowledge, truth, and strength. Similarly, in our Vedas, it is said: Natasya Pratima Asti Yasyanama Mahatyashah — which means God has no physical form or image; He exists in qualities, which we can embody in our lives. That is why He can reside in living beings, not in lifeless objects like wood, stone, idols, or the earth."

"So that means God exists with life, in our actions and character, but not in all material things. I now understand what it means for Him to be omnipresent, Father!"

They sat quietly for a while, gazing at the twinkling stars in the sky. There was silence in the air. The earth had settled into peace. Perhaps, in the vastness of the cosmos, there was a presence — not only above the universe but also within the hearts of those who wished to love, help others, and hose who held unwavering faith.

As the night deepened, Utkarsh leaned onto his father's shoulder. "Father, do you think God can see us?"

Anand smiled gently. "Yes, perhaps He can. Or maybe He is waiting for us to see Him first, in everything around us... in goodness, in kindness, and in truth. Who knows? Perhaps He, too, is a lonely soul, just like us."

• • • •

9. A Man in Love

Why did I love Sudha at all? Did I love her honestly?

I have my doubts even now. My dilemma about love started right there. I wasn't just her classmate — she was two years older than me. Looking back, I realize I was quite immature then.

Love intertwines with age and body, but I didn't understand it back then. In Sudha's presence, I forgot my own age. If one lets go of the body, what remains of the mind? I believed everything was possible with a strong willpower. So, I was convinced I could make Sudha mine, a life partner.

During college bus rides and picnics, Sudha always reserved the seat next to her — for someone close to her. Outside, it rained. The bus moved through winding roads. Despite the crowded vehicle, she never gave up that seat.

"Can I sit here?" I had asked once.

She glanced at me briefly and immediately picked up her vanity bag from the adjacent seat. The moment I sat down, she pulled out some peanuts from her bag and offered them to me in her cupped hand. There was no hesitation in her touch, no nervousness in her gestures. I couldn't tell if there was love in her eyes or not. That day, I wasn't searching for any physical chemistry between us.

Her silent gaze didn't seek warmth; it sought reassurance—a gentle presence. But did she want my attention only as an infatuation? Even now, I don't have an answer to that.

I wrote poetry every night. The first reader of my unfinished poems was Sudha.

"Poet, didn't you write anything today?" she once asked me. Why not? I showed the write up.

One day, while searching for books in the library, I suddenly found myself face-to-face with her.

"What are you looking for? T.S. Eliot or Tanushree?" she teased.

"I'm looking for critic A.C. Bradley. And who is Tanushree? A new face in the first year? Someone who took admission today?" I asked, pretending innocence.

With a playful glint in her eyes, Sudha had said, "Oh, so you were searching for poetry material and even within the books?"

In reality, I wasn't looking for anything in particular. I had come here for a little morning sunlight—Vitamin D, as they say. This part of the library, facing east, was the best spot for it, especially in Winter.

"Did you get the light?"

"No, I found the sun itself here," I replied, settling into the chair beside the window corner where Sudha always sat. From this spot, one could see the campus entrance gate. Sudha always chose this corner. From here, you could watch the afternoon sun's golden rays scatter over the swaying leaves of the banyan tree in the breeze.

Sundays and holidays felt long and melancholic. Those were the days when meeting Sudha at college was impossible. The entire day at the hostel would feel restless — focusing on studies seemed impossible. Everything felt disorganized. And the next day, after such a long wait, even the briefest moment with her felt precious.

The joy of meeting her was fleeting, but the moments of longing were much more intense! Poetry was written on Sunday nights. In the evenings, I would watch an evening-show movie with friends. We would chat, joke, and pass the time. Sudha had come to a matinee show just once, skipping her CVN Sir's Alfred Tennyson's poetry class. His classes were invariably drab. While her class was in session, many students, including Sudha, would doze off. We termed skipping a class as "bunking," but Sudha called it "dumma."

There were so many things left unsaid between me and Sudha. Maybe due to hesitation or some unknown reason, I, a student of literature, never gathered the courage needed to say them. Perhaps it was for the best — some things remain beautiful when left unspoken. And in that indifferent mindset, I drifted into silence.

"Why such indifference, my friend? Is that what it means to be a man? Perhaps it suits ascetics. But unless you're bold and straightforward, you'll never win the love of a beautiful woman," CVN Sir had once said.

I had never analyzed the situation from such a psychological perspective before. Now the question had surfaced, but no answer was in sight.

The next day was Sunday. The college was closed, but the library remained open.

"You're coming tomorrow, right, Sudha? To the department?" I had asked. She had said yes, and I felt reassured.

"Is it absolutely necessary for me to come?" she had replied, taking three steps forward. Yet, something in her question had already given me a definite answer.

She could have just said "yes." That would have been enough. Instead, she had chosen to say, "We had talked about it, right?" but even that, she hadn't explicitly said.

The next morning felt impossible. After a restless night, I stood in the college courtyard as usual, in front of the library pillar where Sudha always stopped. She would lean against the wall, pressing a few books to her chest, her face calm and unreadable. She wore a light-colored cotton saree over her slender frame. The black strap of her brassiere peeked from behind her saree's pallu. And on her lips, there was a quiet smile.

"Do you have something to say, Malhar?" Sudha's voice was steady yet unmistakably clear.

"No, I've found my answer," I said, though in truth, I had found nothing. Maybe I was only deceiving myself.

"Have you written a new poem? You haven't read one out today."

Sudha reached out her hand. Can a poem truly say everything? Words on paper never capture what lips can express. Symbols and metaphors in poetry often obscure the language of the heart, the raw intimacy of love.

In that moment of impulse, I held her hand. Pressed her soft, red fingertips against my chest. I wanted her to feel my heartbeat—to understand me through touch. Had I transferred my warmth, my emotions, into her palm? Had I inscribed my poem upon her trembling fingers? It was warm. It was fluid.

"Are you mad, Malhar?" she said, withdrawing her hand.

Did this really happen? Or had I only imagined it? Even now, I can't be sure.

The next day, as always, Sudha arrived at 10:30 a.m. sharp.

The poem I had handed to Sudha from my diary—was it truly an expression of my heart? Or was it an obscure piece of writing that layered itself over my emotions, veiling my desires and scattering them in fragments? In the delicate folds of a journal, I had preserved my poem as if I were a poet—something I was not.

"Did you come to college today just to read this poem instead of focusing on your studies?" Sudha had asked.

I couldn't tell her that it wasn't just a poem—it was my simple, unspoken feelings.

Sudha walked away. Forever.

Once the semester exams ended, campus romances dissolved into nothingness. The heart's emotions remained locked within diary pages, turning into poetry. No words were ever spoken of that first thrill, of the early monsoon mornings, of the hostel corridors adorned with freshly bloomed gulmohar flowers.

Seasons passed — summer, monsoon, winter, and spring.

In the ceaseless rush of life, I lost track of how many years had evaporated. Amid the demands of survival, even the dearest of women became distant. New poems were written, woven from future longings. The once-etched letters on the weathered college walls faded under the drizzles of passing monsoons.

•• After four years, I met Sudha again. She had become fuller, more radiant, exuding an undeniable charm. Her lips carried a joyful ease.

She was now a lecturer at a small-town college. For the first time, I felt certain that I could finally voice my truth to her — my long-held, unspoken yearning for warmth and a quiet, dependable bond.

"Congratulations, Malhar, on your new poetry collection," Sudha said.

"Then, I guess you never really lost my address?"

What are you saying! Does an address disappear if there is no letter or phone connection? The world is a very small place. I thought you were a realistic and pragmatic person," said Sudha.

"Rather, many good things remained unsaid between us.... But now, I will speak my heart without hesitation. Agreed?"

"When did I agree? Speak your heart first. Later, I'll decide whether to agree or not."

After some hesitation and internal conflict, I made up my mind to speak. Sudha remained unwavering, with no sign of anxiety. As she looked directly into my eyes, I felt uneasy.

"What I will say is not in poetry, but in prose this time. If you agree to this condition, I'll tell you," I started speaking in one breath. I surprised myself. Love confessions are usually in poetry — there was no such rule, yet I had made a mistake here.

Suddenly, one of Sudha's fellow lecturers entered the room. Sudha immediately stood up and introduced him to me.

"Samir, I told you about my close friend Malhar. He writes good poetry. He's a bank officer in Cuttack."

I'm Samir Mahapatra. I teach history," he said, shaking hands with me.

Sudha looked overjoyed. After a quick glance around, ensuring no one was watching, she leaned close to my ear and whispered something. Its meaning was clear — she loved Samir, for a lifetime.

My hidden desire froze me on the spot — motionless.

— Meeting Sudha suddenly after six years was unimaginable. By then, she was like a weary traveler.

That morning, I was supposed to attend a poetry conference. While having breakfast, someone pushed the door open and entered. I realized it was Sudha.

She sat on the nearby chair, drank tea, and said she had come to review poetry at an event.

"They couldn't find a professional critic across the state, so they had to search for me and bring me here," Sudha said.

I sensed that behind her humility, there was a flicker of self-satisfaction. Pride? Who knows.

"Are you reading poetry today?"

I don't write anymore, and even if I do, it's not for reading in public," I told Sudha.

"Don't you have any old poems?"

"I do. But reading or reciting them now won't feel right. They are personal. I don't want to be exposed to vagaries of weather... like expired medicine after a certain date. Why, will you review my poetry too? Often, I don't understand my own poems... I wonder why was I writing poetry in the first place? To become someone's favorite?"

Was I ever truly Sudha's beloved? Did I ever love her honestly without expecting anything? I don't know.

••••

10. Taming the Mother-in-law

Sulata got married on October 1st. Coincidentally, that day was also her mother-in-law's birthday. As is common in middle-class families, her wedding was grand and extravagant. However, within a year and a half of married life, she realized one thing for certain—she could never truly become her mother-in-law's beloved daughter-in-law. Nor could she ever love her with all her heart.

Before Sulata married Amar, their horoscopes were matched, and out of 36 points, their compatibility scored 30—a supposedly excellent match. But no one had thought of checking her compatibility score with her mother-in-law's. If they had, perhaps this current conflict wouldn't have arisen, leaving her feeling so frustrated.

Hearing her complaints about her mother-in-law, neighbors and acquaintances might consider her disrespectful, selfish, or even arrogant. But only those who put themselves in Sulata's place and experienced her daily struggles could truly understand her situation.

"Every morning, I have to wake up early to do all the household chores—cleaning, washing dishes, and sweeping. If I ever wake up late, even by accident, it's as if I've committed an unpardonable sin. My needs, my health, my menstrual cycles—none of it matters. I am insulted and shamed regardless. Yet, when my noble husband wakes up late at his leisure, no one has any objections."

"Do you have no sense of shame? How dare you compare yourself, a daughter-in-law, to my accomplished son?" her mother-in-law lashed out.

"Mother, have I achieved nothing? Am I inferior to him? I also work—a government job at that! I receive my salary every month directly from the state treasury," Sulata replied.

"Are you seriously comparing your meager government job to Amar's salary of one lakh rupees?!" her mother-in-law scoffed.

"Our office work is difficult too. And besides, I will have a pension after retirement. Your son, though a manager, works in a private company. He won't have any pension at all!" Sulata muttered under her breath, unable to resist the urge to retort.

And then there was the matter of cooking. Amar knew that before marriage, Sulata had never stepped into the kitchen. Yet now, she was expected to cook for the entire household. The housemaid, who had once helped with the cooking, was dismissed right after Sulata arrived.

"Now that we have a daughter-in-law, what's the need for a servant? How much work do we have here for just a few people?" The unspoken rule of middle-class households had trapped her.

Thus, in her in-laws home, Sulata found herself confronting these ingrained middle-class mindsets, struggling to find her place in a household that seemed determined to diminish her.

Last Sunday, Mrs. Maitili visited their home, and Sulata had prepared pakoras for her. However, since the pakoras had a little too much salt, her mother-in-law made a disgusting face and slammed them onto the dining table.

"What is this nonsense? Will you serve such things to guests? Didn't your mother teach you even basic cooking?" her mother-in-law shouted in front of Maitili.

"I tried my best, but the salt turned out to be a little out of proportion ..." Sulata replied meekly.

"Why didn't you check the recipe on Google or YouTube? Back in our time, no one taught us how to cook either!"

"Did you even have YouTube or smartphones back in your time?"

"So what if we didn't? We're old fashioned rustics! We managed to learn recipes from cookbooks, newspapers, and magazines. Since when has cooking become some sort of a rocket science?"

Sulata's busy schedule at the office only added fuel to her mother-in-law's frustration. One evening, when she returned home exhausted at nine o'clock, even Amar seemed irritated.

"Which farewell party lasted this late?" he asked, his tone carrying an unmistakable hint of sarcasm.

"If everyone is happy with me quitting my job, then so be it," Sulata said.

"Are you mad? You want to leave your government job?

Is your brain working properly? Why not just hire a cook?" her mother retorted over phone. Her father-in-law remained silent.

"Even Amar doesn't like me working late at the office. Every day I go to work, so many household chores remain undone. Mother-in-law can't manage everything alone. So, I am thinking of staying home and doing some freelance work instead," Sulata said.

"You think it over about everything at home and decide what's best. I don't interfere in your household matters," said her father. She finally put in her papers explaining a few personal reasons.

Even after quitting her job, Amar, her mother-in-law, and the neighbors assumed that freelancing required neither time, focus, nor effort. So, as long as Sulata handled all the household chores and dedicated only a couple of hours to office work, it was acceptable. Moreover, her earnings should be such that her mother-in-law could proudly flaunt her generosity before friends and neighbors! But her part-time work fetched a paltry few rupees.

Before the Puja festival, Sulata went shopping with Amar. As they were about to leave, her mother-in-law's gaze fell on her dress.

"Is that from your college days? Now that you're the daughter-in-law of this respectable house, do you think it's appropriate to wear college-time dresses outside? What will people say?"

"I'm already running late, Ma... Let me finish shopping first; then I'll listen to all the dress-code lectures meant for a daughter-in-law," Sulata replied.

"There's a rural saying—'Eat as per your taste, dress as per others'.' Cook what you like, but wear what society finds acceptable. If you wear such bright-coloured gorgeous dresses, even strangers will turn to look at you. Some might even pass nasty comments."

"If a stranger turns to look at me, that's their problem, not mine!" Sulata retorted. And so began a new argument with her mother-in-law.

"Can't you just stay quiet in front of Ma for a while? That would solve all your problems," Amar said.

"Why should I stay quiet? Am I not her daughter-in-law?"

"Why? Can't you think yourself as her daughter?" Amar asked.

"When has she ever treated me like her daughter? She gives her daughter a saree worth two thousand rupees, but for her daughter-in-law, it's just five hundred! That's the value?"

"Don't compare yourself to others," Amar said and fell silent.

After finishing their shopping, Sulata was starving. "Shall we grab something to eat at the nearby restaurant?" she asked.

"Are you out of your mind? Why don't we just go home? If we eat outside, the food prepared at home will go waste, and then we'll have to give an explanation to Ma," Amar replied.

Whenever Sulata visited her parents on weekends or holidays, she had to face a barrage of questions from her mother-in-law. "Where were you till now? Whose house did you visit? What did you eat at the hotel? When did you get there?"

Would she have to carry the entire household's burden on her shoulders for the rest of her life? Who knew! She was assigned so many responsibilities that no matter what she did, her mistakes would always be pointed out, she'd be scolded, yelled at... Even her husband, along with the rest of the family, would sometimes taunt her.

"Do you know what happened today? My dear, never ask your wife any such questions. Otherwise, there will be chaos in the house," her mother-in-law would whisper to Amar in Sulata's absence. And if, at that moment, Sulata's mother happened to call, she would be given a graphic description of the incident with some twists.

"Didn't you teach your daughter any manners?" Her mother-in-law would often humiliate her mother.

"Why don't you ever invite your daughter and son-in-law for dinner before the festivals? It would enhance your status. And when they leave, you could at least slip five hundred or a thousand rupees into their hands to ensure a smooth journey. Or, at the very least, couldn't you hand them a box of sweets? That's just basic courtesy. I'm not asking for gold jewelry... It's not like I can't afford it," her mother-in-law would boast to her relatives.

"What exactly do you do all day that leaves you so very exhausted by evening?"

"I'm running the house like a maid—cooking, cleaning, doing everything. On top of my freelancing work, I even help Amar with his office files late into the night."

"Your elder sister-in-law helps with the cooking. How much do you really do?"

Her mother-in-law would always undermine her work, and both she and Amar would blame Sulata for even the smallest mistakes. If Amar forgot to hang his wet towel on the balcony, left the fan running, or rushed out without taking his lunchbox, it was always Sulata's fault. Invariably so.

Amar's 12-13 hour office routine used to be such that he hardly spends any time at home.

"Sulata, where are you? What are you doing? I need you downstairs for something," called out her mother-in-law as she entered Amar's room.

"Go, go... Mother is calling you," said Amar.

"No, I can't get along with her. If I visit a relative's place, she feels jealous. If I go to a movie with you, she has a problem. If we visit my home or my sister's, she suddenly gets diarrhoea or some other ailment—I just don't understand! And you expect me to accept her as my mother? How can I do that pretension? She's trying to take over my entire life... She doesn't let me do anything! My independence is shrinking in this house. I'm going to my parents for a few days," said Sulata.

Whenever Sulata wants to visit her parents, she must seek her mother-in-law's permission. If she refuses, Sulata has no choice but to stay back.

"This time, she won't stop me. I'll inform her and leave," said Sulata in a huff.

"No, you won't do anything like that," said Amar.

For the sake of her husband, father-in-law, and their family, she had to give up her career. And in this household ruled by her mother-in-law, she never received empathy — only endless chores. Instead of appreciation, she faced taunts and mistreatment. How could a woman be happy in such a place?

"Mother, I wanted to talk to you," said Sulata.

"About what?" her mother-in-law asked, turning toward her.

"Yes, Mother," Amar joined in. "My company has finally approved staff quarters for me. So we've decided to move there. We'll be shifting in a couple of days."

"Oh? Why?" asked his mother. "Is this house feeling like a burden? Ask your father... See what he says."

"Yes, Mother. It was Father who advised me to apply for quarters," Amar replied.

Why did you keep me in the dark about the whole episode? Am I the villain of the house? She asked in a bid to conceal her tears.

11. A Call from Home

Who are you? You look like a foreigner. Where is your home? Are you from Bengal? Or a Pakistani infiltrator sneaking in? What business do you have in this village? Are you trafficking bonded laborers abroad from here? Or have you come to gather secret information about our missile launch centre?

Sir, greetings.

Who are you? Greeting me like an acquaintance? And... touching my feet? Step back! Shyamaranjan Sir pulled his feet away from Aniruddha's touch.

Aniruddha, after touching his teacher's feet, took out some sweets from his bag.

"Oh, don't you know I am diabetic? Are you trying to tease me, knowing I don't eat sweets? If my son finds out, he will scold me!"

"Your son is in California; how would he know? Please have some, Sir. Eating sweets doesn't cause diabetes. It's only when the pancreas in the body cannot digest sugar properly that diabetes becomes a problem!"

"Where have you disappeared for so many years? Suddenly how come you remember the village after a decade? And where is your son working now? Is that why you brought these sweets as a bribe? Where have you been all this time?" A playful smile spread across Shyamaranjan Sir's face.

"Yes, it's been years. My son Arnab is now working in Florida."

"How far is Florida from India? Has he ever met my son there?"

"Sir, your son is in California, which is in the western United States, along the Pacific. Arnab is on the east coast, by the Atlantic Ocean. If Arnab takes a flight, it will take him about five hours to reach your son. Your son is more than 2,500 miles away from Arnab."

"Our country is on the shores of the Pacific Ocean. Does that mean we are closer to California and farther from Florida?"

"No, Sir. The Pacific Ocean connects India and America, but the distance between the two countries is at least 8,000 miles. A flight journey takes about 17-18 hours."

"And have you arranged a bride for your son by any chance?"

"Would our children wait for us to make decisions for them? First, they took jobs abroad against our wishes. They studied in government universities in India with scholarships but went to serve another country. The real benefit went to the foreign land!"

"Well, has he sent any money back home?"

"No. If they had invested in a house, the village, or the country, that would have been different. I never expected his money because we never lacked anything. But many poor parents sell their land and homes or take heavy loans to educate their children. If their kids turned out like this, what would happen to them?"

"By the way, did Arnab take any bank loan for his studies?" asked Shyamaranjan Sir.

"Yes, Sir. He took a loan of 15 lakh rupees. With interest, the repayment amount came to nearly 17 lakhs. Arnab managed to pay back about 2 lakhs. I withdrew some money from my retirement fund to clear the remaining debt."

"Does your son provide any financial help to the family?"

"We never expected his help. But once he secured a well-paying job, he should have at least repaid his loan himself."

Yes, you may not expect anything from him. However, he should voluntarily provide some support to the household. I understand that you had a well-paying job, but you have already retired ... Are you receiving your pension on time?

Yes, sir. Just recently, I built a house in Visakhapatnam. Vanaprastha. Near the Rushi Hills by the seashore. A little away from the chaos of the city.

And has your wife come to the village along with you? Or have you left her alone at Visakhapatnam? The teacher asked with a touch of sarcasm.

Sir, if you look closely, even in a crowd, we are all alone. Silent amidst the noise. When I return from my house, no one will go back with me? Whoever is meant to go their own way... My son lives in America. My daughter stays in Delhi. Now, my wife Anita has gone to be with our daughter. Everyone keeps asking, why are we staying there in Visakhapatnam?

So, you've decided to spend your 'Vanaprastha' (concluding) years of life in Andhra Pradesh? That far from Odisha? Shyamaranjan questioned.

Far, Sir? Our children have crossed continents. We are still within the Andhra-Odisha borders. Once upon a time, Odisha and Andhra Pradesh were under the Madras Presidency. Back then, we were enslaved in our own country. Now, our children toil under foreigners. They don't get leave, nor do they have time for family matters or celebrations. When Arnav couldn't come to his sister's wedding from America... if this isn't servitude to foreigners, then what is? He had sent a few hundred dollars for his sister as a wedding gift.

This isn't just your personal problem. It's mine as well. In fact, it's a national issue... My wife wasted away longing for her son. In the end, he couldn't even return from California before she passed away.

You mean he hasn't come home in the past two years? Aniruddha asked.

Not just two years! It's been five. And yet, he tells me, "why are you still stuck in the village? Come to America..." Tell me honestly, am I the one stuck in the village, or is he the one trapped abroad? Here, I till the soil, grow crop and merge with the earth. I worked as a teacher, struggled to get him into IIT, and now he has a job abroad. And suddenly, our homeland is untouchable to him? The Gita says: Swadharme nidhanam shreyah, paradharmo bhayavah. (It is better to die in one's own land, religion or faith than to follow another's faith with fear.)

What does that mean? Is a foreign land Paradharma? Is one's own country Swadharma? Aniruddha asked.

Of course... I think you too, like me, have lost your way somewhere, said Shyamaranjan.

Aniruddha said nothing. He crossed the teacher's house and walked ahead. Everyone has their own destination. Each person's path is shaped by their needs and responsibilities. So, based on what they choose, they are all right in their own way. When will he return from this wandering?

Anita is in Delhi now. She has gone to be with her daughter, and to take care of her grandson. She may come back home, whenever she wants to return to Visakhapatnam. But can she suddenly decide to go to Arnav in the US? If her son and his wife invite her, will she go to Florida? Take a short trip, visit America — if they want her...

But one day, everyone must return home.

After Anita left for Delhi, he became lonely in his own house. Wanting to roam around, he has come to Odisha.

The northern coast of Andhra was drenched in drizzles. Probably a depression-induced rain. He had locked up Vanaprastha and left.

Near Ramanaidu Film Studio, by the Geetam College road, was his quiet home. When he opens the window, he can see a world of birds. The chirping of newborn fledglings on the balcony resonated deep within him. The chicks kept calling out: Mama, Papa! Chirp, chirp...

Who are these birds? He looked up. Through the gaps in the thick foliage, the sky appeared dark.

Unknowingly, he had wandered near the ancient banyan tree by the village cremation ground. Ah, childhood! He was transported back in time. Sir's voice echoed in his mind—how many times had he fallen asleep under that banyan tree?

The coarse hands of time stroked Aniruddha's head in the dead of night. Even now, he could hear the master of the Universe caugh from a distant, eternal cough.

Who was coughing at this hour?

Who?

Himself?

Oh, for a long time, his phone had been ringing—from Florida. Arnav.

"Papa, I'm coming back to India very soon. Due to the third wave of the Pandemic, the company has announced a three-month leave for all its employees. I'm coming because the situation in India is a little better now... Yes, Papa."

What time is it now? He asked.

"It's 1:30 in the afternoon here in Florida. In India, it must be midnight, Papa. Next week, I'll reach Delhi... then I'll go to Visakhapatnam."

"Okay." Aniruddha said.

So, in the morning, he would have to return—to his retreat in the Rushi Valley. Where the baby birds awaited him, despite the persistent drizzle and the biting cold.

12. A Journey Westward

He was close to seventy. Not everyone would guess his age. Either he would settle into an armchair on the balcony and read a newspaper or a book until his eyes gave in to exhaustion, or he would laze under the soft morning sun, lying still with his eyes closed. He had no reason to hurry—there was no office to rush to anymore. These days, he had the luxury of uninterrupted freedom.

The subject of discussion here is a man named Nirakar—formless in name, yet he had a distinct presence. From today, he had thought, he would retire and remain stress-free. But reality had other plans.

"Won't the mountains crumble?" His wife, Manasi, gently chided him. He could hear the delicate footsteps of someone climbing the stairs with a steaming cup of spicy tea.

Everyone indulged in happiness in their own way—some in dreams, some in reality. Nirakar wished to spend his days at home, eating whatever he desired, sleeping until sleep took over, and watching TV until his eyes burned. No more office work, no household chores—just a life of leisure. This was his dream of indulgence.

"Get up, get up!" Mansi woke him up as if performing a morning ritual. "Idlis are coming from the Kerala Hotel.

Finish breakfast and go to a movie or the club—that's your choice."

Nirakar, holding his newspaper, was about to head toward the washroom when Manasi snatched it from his hands.

"Read the news after breakfast, not now."

"Why so many restrictions on reading the newspaper?"

"If you read it in the afternoon instead of the morning, will the news turn stale? A high blood pressure patient shouldn't start the day with the news—it's all negative these days!"

Before retirement, Nirakar was a consultant for a company. As soon as his contract ended, another startup firm expressed interest in hiring him. He had asked for ten days to decide. The salary was high, but the owner had set ambitious profit targets, aiming to double earnings in a short time.

His previous company had offered him something better than money—freedom. His work had given him joy and creativity. Before retiring, he had traveled across western and southern India for work. Now, even those work-related pilgrimages had come to an end.

But was there any pilgrimage more fulfilling than sitting on the balcony, reading the newspaper in a swinging chair? Every now and then, Manasi would bring him homemade tea along with his blood pressure pills. That, too, was a kind of peace.

"Did you hear? The husband and wife are not talking since the morning."

"With you? Why?"

Not with me. With each other. It seems they had an argument last night. Your daughter-in-law left for the office without breakfast, talking about old parents, expenses and our home matters. She didn't even comb her hair properly today.

And what about our son? What was he saying? Did he eat?

No. Probably, he will eat at his office canteen.

Yes, doesn't life need a little break from routine? For a change ? Nirakar spoke casually.

After so many years, this husband has grown old... If the wife suggests a change, what will be the state of the husband?

So, have they made any cooking arrangement for us today?

Babu said that if needed, Papa should get the groceries from the nearby grain store.

So, does that mean I have to go out?

Immediately. Even the housemaid didn't come today, Manasi said.

Shall I help with some household chores? Nirakar asked.

No need. You've provided enough happiness in life. Now just go to the market and get some groceries.

But Nirakar had never heard Manasi openly acknowledge the material comforts he had given her. A good child, wealth, property, a car — she had never explicitly accepted any of it. Well, let it be.

"Is our presence in the house causing any trouble for the children?" he asked.

Manasi remained silent.

Why aren't you saying anything? Nirakar tried to gauge his wife's feelings.

They were discussing whether to rent a house elsewhere, Manasi informed him.

This house is in our son's name, which means we are technically tenants in his home, Nirakar said.

Still, the house was built with your money as capital. Maybe they don't consider it theirs because of that. To get an income tax exemption, they took a housing loan...

So, we got the house registered in our son's name. If it's inconvenient for them, we will rent a separate house nearby and stay there. Why are you getting so worried? for me." "Let it be. There is no need to take up a job and invite more illness. Go to the market and get some groceries.weI'll start cooking once you are back.

Nirakar stepped out of the apartment. No one recognizes a retired employee anymore. Sitting by a roadside shop, he called Sen Gupta. He asked whether his contract renewal had been decided.

"Give me some time. I'll let you know. If you can come to the office for ten minutes..." Sen Gupta said before hanging up.

By then, Nirakar had already reached the bus stop. He had never taken a proper day off despite working tirelessly all his life. He didn't even want to retire.

"Sir, namaste. Have you retired from your job?" his neighbor Ghanshyam asked.

"Yes." No, he shook his head.

Manasi's phone rang. He picked it up reluctantly.

"I knew you'd cause trouble once you left the house," Manasi said.

Nirakar cut the call.

As he entered the office, many familiar faces came out to greet him warmly. He went straight to his old chair. No one had taken it yet.

"Welcome, Nirakar Babu. Glad you came," Sen Gupta said, signaling for him to sit and ordering coffee.

"The management was discussing your retirement. I told them that you are healthy and have already applied for a two-year extension."

"But I haven't applied..."

"Then do it now. Do you want to negotiate any extra benefits?"

"No, sir. I need an accommodation this time."

"Alright. We have a guest house near Patia. The house has two-bedrooms with a kitchen. Fully furnished. Want to stay there? There's a garden too, and a caretaker who is a good cook of meat."

"But we have given up non-veg for two years now."

"There, you won't have to pay for electricity or water either. The company will cover it."

"But why would the company do that?"

"Look, does the company give pensions? You spent your whole life working for them, sacrificing everything. What did you get in return? Blood pressure, diabetes, and stress."

"Same with our children. We spent our whole lives working for them, giving them education, cars, weddings, and homes. And what did we get in return in our old age?"

Nirakar stood up. Shaking hands with Sen Gupta, he walked out.

The security guard, Basanta Sahu, who had been waiting outside the office, suddenly fell at Nirakar's feet.

"Hey, get up! What is this, Basanta?" Nirakar said, startled.

Basanta, his voice choked with tears, pleaded, "Sir, do you remember my son? He needs a job."

"I'm already retired... But fine, I'll speak to Sen Saheb," Nirakar replied, trying to console him.

"I know you're heading back to the office, Sir," Basanta said.

"Yes, I understand your concern," Nirakar said as he turned back.

At home, an eerie silence reigned. His wife, Manasi, looked furious.

"So? What did you do? You were saying you'd just spend your days lying around. And yet, you went out and fixed a job for yourself! Do you even care about your health?" she snapped.

"Who said I'm unwell? I'm perfectly fit!" he retorted, grabbing a newspaper and heading to the balcony.

"Fit? You? The moment a little extra work piles up, you get irritable. If the curry lacks salt, you break glassware in anger. And now, at this age, you've taken up a job again!"

"Enough! Be quiet. Our son is here. Listen to what he has to say," Nirakar cut her off.

"Mom, my office is too far from here. So, we're thinking of renting a house near Patia," their son announced.

Manasi, taken aback, asked, "Then what will we do with this house? Rent it out? Or sell it?"

"No, Mom. We can't sell the house. Not until the bank loan is cleared. Instead, you both should continue living here."

"No," Nirakar said firmly. "Tell him, we are leaving this house."

"Leaving? Where will you go?"

"He's got a new job. Along with that, he'll get a free quarters," Manasi added, connecting the dots.

• • • •

13. The Bond of Attachment

"An old mobile phone, a car, or a house will eventually break down. A wife, children, or relatives will also leave you one day..." Abinash said.

Hearing these words inside the auditorium sent a chill through the listeners.

But Abinash, also known as Swami Manmanabhava, uttered these words as though he had erased all attachments from his own life.

Once, Abinash had been his beloved student. Unlike others who focused on studies, he was more inclined toward gardening, extra-curricular activities and sports. The ability of Swami Manmanabhava to deliver seamless philosophical discourse was beyond the imagination of Headmaster Manasranjan.

"Swamiji, why do we experience sorrow in life? What is the cause of suffering?" asked an eager listener.

Swami Manmanabhava smiled and replied, "First, answer my question."

"Yes, ask me," the listener said.

"Name a person or thing you love most in life?" he said. "That very person or object is the cause of your suffering.

When they leave your life, your sorrow begins to afflict you. The life you love so dearly is itself the root cause of your pain. You must have noticed how much it hurts when someone close to you speaks harshly. This is sorrow linked with attachment."

Hearing about loved ones leaving, something stabbed deep into Manasranjan's heart. Two years had passed since his wife's death. In that time, his children had completely forgotten their mother. Let alone his grandchildren.

But Manasranjan had not been able to free himself from the emotional pull of his wife's presence. He cooked, ate alone, managed the household, and continued his school duties. Yet, amidst all this, he never forgot her presence. He could still feel every breath she had once taken.

A deep loneliness had engulfed him — 24/7, day and night. He often mumbled to himself, sometimes even whispering as if talking to someone unseen. The doctor had called it "obsessive-compulsive depression."

"You can call it attachment or illusion," Swami Manmanabhava had said. "If we don't free ourselves from this, we hinder the liberation of our loved ones' souls."

"The body dies, but the consciousness of a person does not as he carries it forward into the next life," he continued. "Sri Aurobindo said that the soul does not perish. One death does not end life. It is merely a journey from one home to another."

"The Bhagavad Gita says the body perishes, but the soul does not. A soul bound by worldly attachments lingers near its body during cremation. It returns to the place where it kept its wealth or spent its life. If, within ten to twelve days, it doesn't overcome its attachments, it remains trapped in the mortal world instead of moving toward liberation. The Garuda Purana speaks of this..."

No, he had to return home early. His three sons were arriving today. Making some excuse, Manasranjan left the gathering.

Three months from now, he was all set to retire. The government had already sent a retirement notice to him. Preparing his pension papers would take another three months.

And then? What remains may be nothing but an empty life. Trapped within four walls, a silent, stagnant existence.

How would he spend his time alone in the old tiled-roof house of the village? His wife, Namita, who had left him two years ago, had still not completely let go of him. Was she still watching over him like a guardian angel? Or had she finally found her path to liberation in the subtle world?

Had she turned into a restless spirit, lingering over the house? No, by now, she might have reached another realm.

According to Swami Abinash, liberated souls move upward, dressed in white light rays, free from all bonds. Their radiant, subtle bodies ascend toward the crimson glow of the divine galaxy called Paramdham. Buddha termed it as Nirvandham or Shantidham.

"When we shed tears for those who have departed, their liberation and upward journey come to a halt. They come to be entangled with the earth's bonds. Evil spirits may also capture them," the former student had said.

As he reached home, a large vehicle was parked at the entrance. It had to be his eldest son's government-assigned car. A chair was placed in the garden. Two of his sons were engrossed in their mobile phones while the eldest had already opened his laptop at the table.

As Manasranjan stepped into the house through the garden, all three sons approached to touch his feet.

"How are you, Baba? Is your health okay?" asked the middle son. The youngest hardly spoke.

"Baba, the roads have become terrible! Odisha has seen no progress in the last twenty years," the eldest son remarked, giving a slight nod before walking away.

Respect, reverence for elders, and traditional values—his sons had inherited these well from their mother.

"Have you eaten something?" he asked and turned toward the dining area. Three plates were on the table, with some food half-eaten and left untouched.

No one waited for him to join them at the meal.

He sighed and looked at the empty chair across him. It still held the presence of someone he could never forget.

According to Abinash Swami, celestial beings seek liberation. They are upward-moving, clad in white garments. They cannot remain confined to a particular place. Free from worldly attachments, the bonds of material desires and affection break away from their ethereal bodies. Their subtle forms, radiating light, dissolve into the infinite. In the path of transcendence, they move toward a crimson glow.

None of the children has acquired the habit of washing dishes and utensils. Namita had left behind a legacy—

not of wealth, but of discipline—having raised her children like little kings while she played the role of a humble servant.

Now, the children must assume that the household servants will take care of the dishes. While Namita was alive, her husband and children lived in comfort. But now, they all seemed to have forgotten that their mother was the one who tirelessly managed everything, providing unwavering service.

She was gone now—defeated by death, reduced to dust. Perhaps she now watched from some ethereal realm, transformed into a divine presence, a mere point of light.

Manasranjan lifted the unwashed dishes from the dining table. The food on the plates had dried up. He placed the utensils in the sink, realizing that there were no servants to help him—something his children never understood. Since Namita's passing, none of them had time to consider who would cook, clean, and maintain the household for their father.

After his retirement, where would he live? Who would take responsibility for him? Who would care for his aging body? He had called his children to discuss these matters. But now that they were all gathered, he thought, why spoil the moment? Instead, he busied himself in the kitchen.

When Namita was alive, she used to prepare tamarind soup because the children loved tangy food. She made banana fritters and chutney with mashed bananas. With steaming rice, they ate without a fuss. But now, in her absence, what would he cook? What would his children eat for dinner? These questions troubled him.

To depend on others was to be indebted. In a worldly sense, it was a burden. And to repay that debt, one had to be reborn in this mortal world over and over again—this was what Abinash Swami always said.

Thirteen days after her passing, where did her astral body go? Manasranjan had forgotten to ask. If Namita's departure to the afterlife was truly certain, then why had she spent her entire life cooking, cleaning, and washing clothes in a schoolteacher's household? Was this what people called fate? A life of sacrifice? An ideal marriage?

Night crept in slowly.

As Manasranjan scrubbed the blackened frying pan by the sink, he felt a presence behind him. He could hear the soft rhythm of someone's breath. A gentle touch brushed against his back. He turned suddenly—no one was there.

A short distance away, his elder son walked away in silence, saying nothing.

A little later, his younger son arrived.

"Baba, hasn't the maid come? Get up. I'll take care of this. You should just focus on cooking. Otherwise, I can bring something from a nearby hotel. You don't need to trouble yourself."

"No, I can't eat outside food. I can't tolerate onions, garlic, oil, or spicy dishes. I'll cook at home in the pressure cooker. Dinner will be ready in forty minutes," Manasranjan replied.

Children grow up so fast—like tall trees. They grow beards, their once-thin voices deepen. They become so large that embracing them becomes difficult.

His younger son freed him from the sink, cleaning the dishes. Two others joined in, helping with the vegetables. Dinner was ready — simple curry and chapatis.

Manasranjan never mentioned the reason he had called the brothers together. Nor did the children dare to ask. Silence filled the air as the night passed.

The three brothers woke up early, preparing to return to their respective homes. But Manasranjan was nowhere to be seen. They waited, hoping he would return from his morning walk and say goodbye.

But he didn't come back.

Growing impatient, the eldest son called him. "Baba, we're leaving now."

"Yes, alright, you all may go," Manasranjan replied from Abinash Swami's ashram. His voice wavered, as though he had already made his decision about his path ahead.

•••

14. The Night in Hostel No. 7

Only four girls remained in the hostel No.7 that night. The annual examinations were over, and most students had already left for their villages before the summer break. But Kanchan and three others had to stay back — their science practicals were yet to be completed.

That evening, the hostel was eerily silent. The warden had gone on leave, and no staff was around. Outside, the night carried the usual drunken echoes from distant corners of the town.

Kanchan — a name given here to protect her real identity for social reasons — was unmarried. What happened that night should never have happened. Yet, it did.

The hostel itself will remain unnamed. Revealing it would be the same as revealing Kanchan's village, her clan — her entire existence.

The discerning reader may already sense the gravity of the event. This was a hostel meant for tribal students, a protected space. And yet, protection was an illusion.

That night, the four girls sat on the veranda, studying under the dim glow of a flickering tube light. As the hours passed, one by one, they retired to their rooms.

Kanchan entered the shared washroom, splashing water on her face, trying to shake off the exhaustion. She returned to her room, bolted the door from inside, changed into her nightwear, and switched off the light.

Just as she was about to lie down, a voice called out from the corridor.

"Kanchan…"

A soft knock followed.

She hesitated. The voice was familiar—probably Mandira, her hostel mate.

Still drowsy, she unlatched the door without a second thought.

The moment the door swung open, a powerful hand shoved it aside. A dark figure lunged in, his body reeking of sweat and liquor.

Before she could react, the intruder grabbed her wrist, twisting it with a force that made her gasp.

A scream rose in her throat, but it never made it past her lips.

A single push, and she was pinned onto the cot. The room spun around her. The weight pressing down on her body was unbearable.

Kanchan's mind raced. She had read about self-defense techniques—how to resist, how to fight back.

Bite him. Scratch his face. Gouge his eyes. Kick his groin. Grab anything—a pen, a pin, even a toothbrush—stab it into his skin.

But she did nothing.

Not because she didn't want to.

Because she couldn't.

The man was too strong. His grip crushed her like a vice.

The struggle ended before it even began.

When she woke up, it was already morning.

She wasn't in her hostel room anymore.

The pale white walls, the antiseptic smell—she was in a hospital bed.

A police officer stood nearby. A lawyer. The hostel warden. A few classmates. And a stack of papers placed before her, demanding her signature.

She stared at them, disoriented. Her body ached, her mind fogged with the remnants of horror.

She signed where she was told, without reading a single word.

Then came the court summons.

Kanchan had never stepped inside a courtroom before. Now, she was being placed in the witness stand.

She wasn't the accused.

But she was the one on trial.

The judge was a man.

The prosecutor was a man.

The court clerk—a man.

Even the peon who kept entering the room on one excuse or another, a man.

Kanchan was told the hearing would be private. Yet, everything in that courtroom felt exposed.

The defense attorney smirked as he questioned her.

"So, you opened the door voluntarily?"

She hesitated. Yes, she had.

"Did the man push his way in? Or did you invite him?"

Her fingers clenched into fists.

"You were in a ladies' hostel. Did you not suspect a man's voice?"

She swallowed hard. Her voice came out weak.

"He called my name... I thought it was my hostel mate."

The lawyer leaned forward, voice dripping with false sympathy.

"And this hostel mate... was she there when he entered?"

"No."

A pause. Then the fatal question—

"So, how do we know this was truly an assault?"

The silence in the courtroom was deafening.

Kanchan felt her breath hitch. The words she needed to say burned inside her, yet she knew—they would never be enough.

Because in that room, surrounded by men in black coats, the truth was nothing more than a puzzle piece that didn't fit.

And she...She was just another statistic.

Kanchan stood rigid in the witness box, her fingers clenched into tight fists. The courtroom smelled of old wood and ink, the slow whir of the ceiling fan doing little to break the thick air of judgment.

The defense attorney adjusted his black coat, his sharp eyes locking onto hers.

"What were you doing in your room at midnight?"

Kanchan's voice was barely above a whisper. "I had just turned off the lights and was about to sleep."

"Then how did you see the man in the dark?"

She swallowed hard. "The veranda light was on. He entered from there."

A flicker of amusement crossed the lawyer's face as he leaned forward. "And then?"

"He grabbed the edge of my saree... I pulled it back."

"And?"

"He pushed me onto the cot and tried to yank my saree away."

A ripple passed through the courtroom. The lawyer tapped his pen against the desk, pacing slowly.

"What did you do?"

"I resisted... I tried to scream, but he pinned my mouth shut with his hand."

The lawyer smirked. "Did you file an FIR with the police?"

Kanchan hesitated. "I think so... I don't remember clearly."

"When he pushed you, did you fall hard enough to get bruised?"

"No... Only my watch broke."

"Did you try to escape?"

"Yes, but he overpowered me."

The lawyer's eyes gleamed. "After pinning you down, what did he do?"

Her fingers trembled. "He... pulled at my saree."

"Did he remove your blouse?"

"No."

"How was your saree draped? Like a Marathi woman's or an Odia woman's?"

Kanchan's voice turned cold. "Odia style."

"Did the accused bite you?"

"No."

"Did you bite him?"

"No."

"How long did the entire act last?"

Kanchan's throat tightened. "Ten... fifteen minutes."

"Did you speak to him at any point?"

"No."

The lawyer's voice dropped to a near whisper, a sinister edge creeping in.

"I wonder... if you truly resisted, could he have succeeded?"

A shiver ran down Kanchan's spine. She knew what he was implying.

Her voice was steady when she answered, "For a beast, nothing is impossible."

The lawyer smirked, unfazed. "Had you seen him before? Did you know him?"

"No."

"After the incident, was there blood on your thighs or private parts?"

Her breath hitched. "I... I don't know. When I regained consciousness, I was in the hospital."

"Did the accused have any mud or dirt on his body?"

"I don't remember."

"What was he wearing? A dhoti or pants?"

"I don't recall."

The questions kept coming, each one slicing through her dignity.

"Did any other part of your body bleed?"

"No."

"Was there any semen on your saree, thighs, or anywhere else?"

"I don't know."

"Did you feel any burning sensation afterward?"

She hesitated. "I... I can't say."

"And after that?"

"I cried."

Silence wrapped the courtroom like a suffocating shroud.

Kanchan's eyes burned, but she refused to let the tears fall. This wasn't just an interrogation. It was another violation—this time, sanctioned by the law.

The trial was over. But the real verdict had already been written long ago.

When the judge finally spoke, his words were cold, detached, and mercilessly precise.

"Based on circumstantial evidence, it appears that there was an attempt at sexual assault. However, the medical report confirms that the victim's hymen remains intact. Therefore, this does not legally qualify as rape—only an attempt."

The words struck like a hammer.

Kanchan stared at the judge, at the lawyer, at the system that had just reduced her trauma to a technicality.

She knew, at that moment, that she would never seek justice again.

Because in this world, justice was only for those who survived not just the crime, but the trial itself.

• • • •

15. Sipra's Poetic Justice

Is it lodged in something tangible, like wood or stone? You wouldn't be able to tell. But one could easily guess her age—twenty-eight.

A mere glance at her face, whether glowing with joy or shadowed by sorrow, offers a glimpse into her mind. Unlike a stone underfoot, which can be seen, touched, and felt, her mind remains elusive. And yet, Sipra herself can be felt—through her words, her actions, the gentle cadence of her voice.

Lately, Sipra has been an enigma. Her hair is neatly styled, her saree draped to perfection, her nails polished, and her lips tinted with just the right shade. Yet, she does not appear radiant. Something is missing. Why?

Even if her brain were dissected, every vein and nerve mapped with precision, would one truly uncover the mystery hidden behind her thalamus—the seat of her subconscious?

"Doctor, can I observe Sipra's surgery?" Animesh asked.

"Why?" The doctor raised an eyebrow.

"I want to see if our shared moments—our hostel walks, our campus conversations—have been registered in her memory the way they are in mine."

The specialist responded, "Do you understand MRI mapping?"

"MRI?" Animesh was puzzled.

"Magnetic Resonance Imaging," the doctor explained. "A technique that captures electromagnetic resonance within the body, mapping internal conflicts and trauma. You might think it's simple, but it's far from it."

Animesh still didn't understand why Sipra needed a brain scan. In a quiet voice, he finally said, "I love you, Sipra... I love you very much."

"Oh, really?" She looked at him, expression unchanged. "You barely know me. Love doesn't just happen like that."

Her face remained impassive, offering neither acceptance nor rejection.

Perhaps she thought, What even is love? So many men in college utter these words, but once examinations end, their affection vanishes into thin air. Sipra had long learned to translate such confessions for what they were — mere illusions.

Is love of the body or beyond it? Is it physical or purely emotional?

How credible is love when it disregards the body and exists solely in the mind?

Sipra didn't answer Animesh's question. She simply turned and walked out of the campus gates.

"At least have a coffee with me before you go," Animesh pleaded.

She ignored him and left.

Sipra knew the perils of letting someone trespass into her inner world. A single careless step could leave muddy footprints on her mind's courtyard. Why should she make it so easy?

She recalled the Bhagavad Gita:

"Yad bhaavam tad bhavati..." This Sanskrit phrase enlarges the idea that our thoughts and beliefs shape our reality. If you desire love, you will find someone to cherish. If you crave wealth, opportunities to earn will manifest. If you hunger, food will appear.

So what did that mean? That one should focus their thoughts on a singular, unwavering truth.

But where does this supreme truth reside? In the sky? Beneath the earth? Among the sun and moon?

"Not in a place," Sipra had once said. "Focus on a point of light. Free yourself from desire. Be still. Only then will you find clarity."

"You mean... like the God Particle?" Animesh had asked, intrigued. "If I fix my gaze on your eyes, will I find it?"

"Not the eyes," she corrected. "Higher. Between the brows. Where the mind dwells, behind the thalamus."

"Who told you about the thalamus?" Animesh pressed. "Then tell me, where is the heart?"

"You're a science student, and yet you ask about the heart?" Sipra smirked. "The heart is nothing but a muscular pump, circulating blood. If it stops, so do you."

"Then what about all those love stories?" Animesh challenged. "Are they all lies?"

"Not lies. The heart is simply a metaphor for human emotions."

The specialist interrupted. "Mr. Animesh, have you ever noticed any traumatic behavior in Sipra?"

Animesh hesitated. "Trauma?"

"Has she ever been unusually harsh or erratic with you?"

"Yes... many times," he admitted. "But why?"

The doctor sighed. "When a person has suffered severe physical or psychological trauma in childhood, their mind becomes defensive—sometimes even cruel. Women, in particular, develop hysterical tendencies if they've been victims of deep-seated abuse, especially..."

He paused.

"...if they have been subjected to something horrific in their youth."

Animesh suddenly remembered. Sipra had once mentioned spending three years in a rehabilitation center due to a childhood incident—something she never spoke about in detail.

And now, everything made sense.

Sipra was only fourteen when Alok, a classmate of her elder brother, extended a hand of friendship toward her. But beneath the guise of camaraderie, he infiltrated the deepest, most sacred corners of her being.

She never forgave him. Not then, not ever.

There were rumors of a dark well in Kashi, a pit of despair swallowing everything whole. But Sipra had already lived through that abyss in her own adolescence.

At the time, she lived at her maternal uncle's house, studying in a town far from home. From an early age, she had suffered mental unrest due to her fractured family life.

Her elder brother and his friends often gathered in her uncle's room to study, and among them was Alok—a mathematics prodigy, well-liked, and trusted. He naturally took it upon himself to tutor Sipra.

But what seemed like innocent mentorship turned into something else entirely.

On quiet evenings, beneath the flickering glow of a lantern, Alok would hold her chin as he explained algebraic equations. Sipra, frozen in place, could no longer hear the numbers. Could no longer see the pages. Her heartbeat thundered in her ears.

Then came the fair at Vishuva Sankranti. In a bustling crowd, where the scent of ripe bananas, black pepper, honey, and bhang infused the air, Alok handed her a glass.

"Just taste it once. See? I'm drinking too," he said smoothly, raising his own glass to his lips.

Sipra hesitated, but then—she drank.

She didn't remember much after that. Just that, at some point, her eyelids had grown impossibly heavy.

She awoke sometime in the night. Her body felt strange, a dull ache running through her limbs. She wasn't in bed. She wasn't even on the floor.

She was sprawled across a wooden cot on the veranda, barely clothed.

And then she felt it.

Alok's fingers, trailing over her skin. Slipping into forbidden places. Trespassing where they had no right to be.

Her body wasn't hers anymore.

"You're dreaming, Sipra. You're flying," Alok whispered into her ear.

She couldn't breathe. She couldn't move. But she could feel. And she felt everything.

She didn't know when she passed out again.

When morning arrived, she opened her eyes to a cruel realization—her innocence lay in ruins. A beast had fed on her through the night, drinking from her like a parasite.

Then, as if bitten by a viper, she bolted upright and screamed.

In a frenzy, she kicked, punched, clawed—until Alok was knocked off the cot, sprawling onto the floor.

"You bastard!" she spat, pulling up her torn frock and wrapping herself in whatever shreds of dignity remained.

Alok staggered to his feet, hands raised in surrender. "I swear, I'll never do this again. Please don't tell anyone."

Sipra glared at him, her fury sharper than broken glass. "Tell anyone?" she echoed. "Why should I? I don't need to. But if you ever try this again, I will show you what real suffering looks like."

Alok gulped. He nodded. "I won't. Never."

"Good," she whispered.

And then, in one swift motion, she moved.

A flash of silver. A blur of motion.

Alok's body jolted as he let out a strangled cry. He clutched between his legs, collapsing onto the ground, writhing in agony.

A crimson pool spread across the wooden floor, drop by drop.

Sipra stood over him, gripping the bloodstained scissors in her trembling hand.

She leaned down, her voice ice-cold. "You won't tell anyone either."

And Alok?

He never did.

• • • •

16. Graft Case Against Surya Mishra

The knock on the door was soft, and almost hesitant. Surya Mishra looked up from his half-packed suitcase. The brass clock on the wall ticked past 7. p.m. It was the last day of his 35-year-long career as a government officer. Retirement was supposed to feel liberating. Instead, his drawing room was now swarming with Vigilance officers.

Bundles of cash—neatly bound, with Reserve Bank seals intact—were strewn across the table. Hidden compartments of almirahs had given way to brick-thick wads. The inspector read from a seizure list, voice clipped and practiced. "The total cash recovered so far is ₹3.42 crore, Sir. Would you like to make a voluntary statement?"

Surya Mishra didn't respond. His throat was parched. He stared blankly at the currency notes as if they belonged to someone else. He watched silently at a photograph of Lord Jagannath on the wall tilted slightly. In the next room, his wife Lata sat on the edge of their bed, her eyes a pool of disbelief and betrayal.

Later that night, after the Vigilance officers had left— having pasted a sealing order on the gate—Lata finally broke the silence.

"You always claimed integrity was your inheritance," she said, her voice trembling. "What happened to that?"

Surya swallowed hard. "It's a trap," he said. "Jealous colleagues. They planted it to disgrace me before I signed out."

Lata didn't blink. "Then why did you walk into their trap?"

He looked away. "I don't know. Maybe I believed. I deserved it for decades of silent service.

"Punished?" she said. "For what?"

He paused. "For trusting the system. For not resisting when temptation knocked. For... forgetting I wasn't invincible."

Lata's voice turned sharp. "Was it also God's plan when you were promoted last year? When your face appeared in newspapers? When people touched your feet outside temple gates?"

Surya's expression darkened. "Of course. As per the Bhagabat Purana, He is both the doer and the punisher. Whatever happens — good or bad — is under His command.

She stood up now, crossing her arms. "Then why act at all? Why not let life flow without effort, if God decides everything?"

His shoulders slumped. "We act. But our actions are often coloured by ego, greed, fear. In the end, karma catches up."

"So did you walk in His Srimat all your life, or just used His name when things went wrong?"

The words struck like a blade.

Lata picked up a framed photo of their younger selves. "You built this house with honest dreams. You sent our son abroad with pride. And now? You'll become a front-page scandal."

Surya suddenly looked older, crumbling under unseen weight. "I didn't take the money for pleasure. I didn't hoard it in Swiss banks. I gave in, yes, in moments of weakness. Maybe I believed I deserved it for decades was owed for decades of silent service."

"Is that your justification?" she asked.

"No," he said quietly. "It's my confession."

The next morning, headlines screamed: Top Bureaucrat Nabbed With Unaccounted Crores On Retirement Eve. The news channels feasted on it. Pundits debated corruption. Ex-colleagues distanced themselves. His pension was frozen. His son in Boston called — humiliated and heartbroken.

But Lata surprised everyone. She didn't leave him. She didn't hide. She began visiting temples more frequently, sometimes alone, sometimes dragging Surya along."

One evening at the Lingaraj Temple, amidst the ringing of bells and smell of camphor, she said, "If God truly governs all, then He must have a reason for dragging you through fire."

Surya replied, "Or maybe He's giving me a last chance to clean my ledger."

The following week, Surya quietly visited a lawyer. Then another. Then a retired investigative officer turned RTI (Right to information) activist.

Three months passed. The Vigilance case appeared stagnant. But Surya had found something.

Inside a tattered blue file from 2013, buried in the Revenue Records Division, lay a transfer order — of a tribal village's forest land to a private mining company. Surya's signature was missing from the final draft. Yet, his name appeared in the approval chain. He remembered: He had resisted that order and was mysteriously transferred overnight to a Kalahandi district.

"I said no," Surya told Lata that night, holding the file. "They bypassed me and forged my initials on annexure pages."

"Who are 'they'?"

"The same men who rose higher than me. Who envied my final promotion. Who feared what I might reveal after retirement."

Lata sat up, stunned. "You mean... you were silenced preemptively?"

He nodded. "And framed, just in time."

Driven by a renewed sense of purpose — or divine rage — Surya started filing RTIs, collecting paper trails, finding contradictions, hidden memos, and minutes of meetings doctored in hindsight. Aided by a young investigative journalist, he built a dossier. At night, he quoted Bhagavad Gita:

"Karmanye vadhikaraste..." You have the right to action, not its fruits.

It all built up to one stormy August evening.

A public hearing was being held by a retired High Court panel on corruption cases stonewalled by bureaucracy. Surya limped to the podium with a brown envelope in hand. He asked for 10 minutes.

He spoke not just about himself, but about a chain of corruption going back 15 years. Names of officers. Kickbacks routed via NGOs. Audio clips. Notarized statements. Stamped receipts. Photos. And finally—a video of a Vigilance officer admitting off record that he was "told to act on Surya Mishra before he got loud."

The hall went quiet.

The moderator, Justice R.K. Rath, a man known for his intolerance toward vendetta politics, demanded immediate protection for Surya and ordered a fresh probe.

Three weeks later, the Vigilance case against Surya Mishra was dropped citing "inconclusive evidence and violation of procedural integrity."

The same news channels that vilified him now showed his photo again—this time with the words: Exonerated. Exalted.

Back home, Surya opened the window and looked out at the garden. Rain touched the leaves, like forgiveness.

Lata brought him a cup of tea. "So... was it still God's plan?"

He smiled faintly. "Maybe. Maybe God wanted me to see what I had become. To stand in the fire. To not burn. To speak."

She touched his shoulder. "Then perhaps this wasn't your retirement. It was your rebirth."

He whispered, almost to himself, "This time, I will walk His path. Not just quote Him from Bhagabat."

Outside, thunder rolled again. But this time, Surya Mishra felt no fear.

• • • •

www.ingramcontent.com/pod-product-compliance
Lightning Source LLC
Chambersburg PA
CBHW011223120626
46545CB00010B/3132